Peter Lewis

THE WAY TO THE
MARTIAL
ARTS

Marshall Cavendish

For Danny Connor
'who gave the spark that kindled the flame'.

Editor: Rachel Stewart
Designer: Glynis Edwards
Production Controller: Richard Church. 1

Published by
Marshall Cavendish Books Limited
58 Old Compton Street
London W1V 5PA

© Marshall Cavendish Limited 1986

Second impression 1990

ISBN 0 86307 558 4

Printed and bound in Portugal

Title page *Sensei K. Enoeda, Chief Instructor of the European
Karate Federation and the Karate Union of Great Britain.*

CONTENTS

INTRODUCTION

Violence has been an inescapable fact of human life since the beginning of time. It is reasonable to suppose, therefore, bearing in mind human ingenuity, that self-defence systems were devised at a very early stage in order to ensure survival of the species. Indeed, man's combat skills have been undergoing a constant evolution. Each addition, by way of another thought-out movement, aided the struggle against aggressors and began to form the basis of a martial skill. Slowly and gradually, mostly through trial and error, fighting became more of an exact science rather than just pure animal instinct.

Murals in tombs along the Nile and hieroglyphics engraved in the pyramids prove that the Egyptians had an organized type of unarmed boxing as early as 3,500BC. For more complete information on a formalized system of combat we must look to the ancient Greeks. The works of Homer (*c.* 9th century BC) contain descriptions of unarmed combat, and the Greek philosopher, Plato (*c.* 428-348 BC), mentions skiamachia, a sort of shadow boxing, which was eventually combined with wrestling to form an art called pancration meaning 'game of all powers'. A wide variety of techniques was allowed. So far as is known, pancration was the first recorded fighting discipline that incorporated a method of kicking with punches and empty-hand strikes. This art, or sport as it should be correctly termed, was introduced into the Olympic Games in 648 BC. Indeed, some people believe that we should regard Alexander the Great (356-323 BC) as the founder of martial arts, who, through his invasion of India, brought with him the unarmed combat method of the Greeks. However, it would seem somewhat presumptuous to suppose that Asia had to wait for that Macedonian conqueror to invade her borders before the martial arts were born. Recent archeological investigation in southern China has unearthed paintings and artifacts suggesting that unarmed fighting methods were in operation long before his time.

Combat is identified with fighting and killing and yet, through the practice of martial disciplines, exponents have found increased spiritual awareness. Thus a strange paradox began to emerge with a concept of inner peace beyond fighting. Ultimately, through continued studies, a search for a higher understanding of one's self could be fostered. No one can train in a martial art discipline without at some stage becoming aware of this fundamental theme. To realize this, is to be halfway towards grasping what martial arts really are.

Today's martial artists begin their training for many different reasons. Some, because it seems a perfect vehicle for reaching a level of physical fitness, others train because the martial arts offer a way of self-protection in these violent times, with muggings becoming commonplace. No matter what the reasons, all start the journey evenly. It is up to each individual to ascertain how far he or she wants to step. Each person has a separate goal to fulfil; the martial arts offer guidance along a special route for those who wish to follow it.

The late seventies and early eighties gave the martial arts a new impetus. As more and more people enrolled in the newly established clubs, it was apparent that the traditional martial arts would be brought into the competitive sporting arena. Within a few short years westerners had gained supremacy on the world tournament scene. Amazingly they surpassed their eastern counterparts in contest, and yet Asia had been the birthplace of the martial arts. However, one cannot help wondering whether somewhere along that road the westerners, with all their emphasis on the sporting aspects, either missed or forgot the old values and true meanings of the traditional Oriental martial arts.

This book is not aimed at the skilled martial arts practitioner, but primarily the interested amateur. It is by no means an in-depth source for serious study, but merely a guide to the extraordinarily wide variety of martial skills practised the world over. It is to be hoped that browsing through these pages will encourage the novice to take up this or that particular style, and by doing so will open up a whole new way of life.

Left A classic karate mae-geri (front kick) to the face. The striking area is the ball of the foot, so the toes must be raised upwards and the foot extended. Much of the power behind this kick comes from the forward motion of the hips.

9

THE MARTIAL LEGACY OF CHINA

'Without ascending the mountain, one cannot judge the height of heaven.'

It was generally accepted that the nucleus of the martial arts was formed when the Indian monk Bodhidharma made an epic trek across the Himalayas to arrive ultimately at the Song Shan Shaolin monastery in the province of Hunan; he brought with him a system of exercises devised to assist his monks in their rigorous programme of work and meditation. However, later research indicated that the martial arts were already blossoming in China long before that legendary journey. Recent findings offer the distinct possibility that a primitive martial art form reached the East via the Fertile Crescent in Mesopotamia, to be later developed by the Indians and the Chinese. There is a Babylonian plaque in the British Museum dating back 5,000 years or more, depicting figures fighting, using systemized blocking and countering techniques.

The general term given to the martial arts of Chinese origin is kung fu. This is really a gross misrepresentation; kung fu simply translated means skill, time spent, strength or ability, or even hard work. It is a period of time utilized by a person to perform a specific type of task. The term was later bastardized in the West and then accepted in the East, to refer generally to the practice of Chinese martial arts. It is also known as gung fu in Cantonese. The correct term should perhaps be wu shu, meaning war arts. This can be loosely employed to encompass all martial arts, though today it is used primarily to denote the form being developed in the People's Republic of China. Wu shu tends to be highly gymnastic—a somewhat diluted version of the original warrior way concept.

The secret tradition

Much of what was learned about the martial arts was handed down by word of mouth only and was shrouded in myth and secrecy. The ancient masters did not reveal their knowledge readily. Only students who were truly dedicated were allowed to glimpse into the techniques of the particular style that the master was teaching, and this was only after their sincerity and absolute devotion to the art had been thoroughly tested.

Through a long series of both difficult and menial tasks the master would ascertain how seriously the budding devotee intended to study his school's particular style of martial art. This early form of character analysis worked very well indeed, and rarely was a master ever let down by a student he had tested. Even today in certain schools of martial arts, this age-old system for accepting only really dedicated students is still practised. Students have often waited years before being allowed the honour to train in even the most basic of techniques. Once accepted, they were bound to a code of secrecy and silence, and were forbidden to share with outsiders the wisdom and knowledge gained from their martial arts training.

Additionally, because of the political intrigue in China, and constant power struggles between the generals and court politicians, practice of the martial arts was often concealed from the authorities, and daily training was carried out behind the confines of the temple walls.

When the head of a martial system knew that either through old age or illness his years were numbered, a search would begin among the senior students for a successor to carry on the style after the master's death. The advanced techniques would then be taught to that chosen person, so that the finer points could be perpetuated. If it should happen that the chosen disciple did not meet the master's requirements, the all-important central core would be withheld and would die with the master, leaving

Left A typical pose from the system known as Shaolin Fists. This hard-soft style of kung fu is believed to have originated at the Shaolin temple in China. The practitioner here adopts a side-on defence to cover vulnerable parts of his body.

behind only a shallow outline of a once great system.

In some forms of the martial arts, the core techniques were committed to handwritten scrolls and handed down from master to senior student. Although on the surface this would seem to be a more reliable way to preserve techniques, one or two indecipherable words could be misinterpreted by the senior student and could multiply over the centuries until that particular style of kung fu had altered quite considerably, perhaps beyond recognition from its original concept. Along the way, the style's effectiveness, combat reliability and philosophical thought could well be lost.

Buddhist and Taoist influences

In China, religion played an important part in the development of the martial arts. Three great religions flourished. There was Confucianism, an austere doctrine of doing the right and proper thing. This mainly aristocratic philosophy found great appeal among the Mandarins and intellectuals but had little to offer the ordinary peasant. Confucianism was based upon the teachings and analects of the Chinese philosopher Confucius. Although not strictly a religion as we in the West accept a religion to be, Confucianism taught duty to parents, devotion to family tradition and dedication to truth and idealism.

The second religion, Buddhism, arrived in China from India. This religion became divided into various sects, until eventually the original Buddhism as practised in India was barely recognizable. One particular branch of Buddhism that was to have a profound effect upon the martial arts became established at the Shaolin temple called Chan; this later gave birth to the Zen Buddhism of Japan. Followers of Chan or Zen believe that the centre for meditation and the seat of mental power is the tan t'ien or tanden, which is a point situated about two inches (5cm) below the navel. In the internal systems of kung fu, it is believed that this is the place where the vital 'chi' energy gathers.

The philosophy of Zen has a deep significance when applied to the martial arts. A beginner enters the place of training with a head full of opinions and thoughts, but part of the discipline is to empty the mind so as to become a vehicle for new learning, in essence to be open-minded. There is a story about an old Japanese Zen master who was engaged in conversation with a prospective student. The student

chatted on and on, full of his own opinions and ideas. He described to the master everything he knew about Zen, trying to impress the old man with his great knowledge. The master sat and listened patiently for a while, then suggested that they take some tea. The student held out his cup dutifully and the master began to pour. The tea came to the top of the cup but still the master kept on pouring. The tea overflowed but still the master kept on. The student, unable to contain himself, pointed out that no more tea would go into the cup. The master looked up and said, 'Like this cup you are full of your own desires and ambitions. How then can I show you Zen unless you first empty your cup?'

To the Chinese peasant the religion they found affinity with was Taoism. The Taoist idea is yielding, or non-action. Its aim is to achieve a peaceful mind without the extremes of either anger or happiness, a mind without worry. Through these ideas, and the exercises that are their material expression, a good, healthy and long life can be achieved. Exercise on a regular basis promotes good health and a healthy body works harder and longer. So the peasant farmers produced a greater yield of crops, thus becoming richer. Although legend suggests that all Chinese martial arts came from Shaolin, it can be seen that in many villages across the country various disciplines which were invaluable to the practice of the arts were already a way of life.

A fundamental teaching of the Taoist religion is that there is a natural harmony of all things, that everything in existence has its complementary opposite. These two opposing forces that flow into one another in a continuous state of change are known as yin and yang, and they are represented by two symbols within a circle. Yin is the negative aspect of the universe and relates to female, night, cold, and it is seen as a black fish with a white eye in the circular diagram. Yang is the positive aspect of the universe indicating the male, day, warmth. It is represented as a white fish with a black eye. Neither can exist without the other. These two inseparable forces are, according to the Taoists, the principle of the universe. The complementary forces flow into one another. Night becomes day, summer becomes winter, hard becomes soft; the yin becomes yang, continually pushing forwards and the yang becomes yin again. These two apparent opposites were not viewed as permanent and irreconcilable, but constantly changing in a ceaseless rhythmic cycle. Understanding this interchange of yin and yang is perhaps the most important single aspect in the learning of a kung fu system.

The yin and yang symbols are surrounded by eight trigrams, which represent the subdivisions of creation, and the sequence in which they are arranged is of importance. It begins with ch'ien, which is the creative principle and seen as heaven, and is represented as three straight yang lines. Its direct opposite is k'un, seen as earth and represented as three broken lines. K'un is the passive principle. The other divisions are lake, fire, thunder, wind, water and mountain. The arrangement of the eight trigrams is attributed to the King Wen, *c.* 1150 BC, and they are employed for divination.

As the Chinese martial arts are all based on either the nature of soft or hard, action or non-action, it can be realized why the philosophy of Taoism played such an important role in their development. Even today the principles of Taoism permeate the martial arts. The country of South Korea, predominantly Buddhist, has as its national flag the yin and yang symbols surrounded by the eight trigrams.

The itinerant priests
Because of conflicts between opposing religions and also because of the Taoist ideal of living close to nature, the priests of old were great travellers. They walked the length and breadth of the country trying to

13

Above In this classical kung fu pose, the leg position is both defensive and offensive. It protects vital points of the body and at the same time is ready to flick out in a kick. Similarly, the arms protect the centreline, yet the hands are ready to strike.

pa lo han sho or 'the 18 hands of the lo han'. Traditionally this eventually became the Shaolin method of Chinese boxing, and the basis of all Shaolin kung fu.

The following centuries saw wandering monks from all over China arriving at Shaolin either as budding disciples or to seek refuge within the temple. Consequently many refinements were added to the existing system of Chinese boxing.

As a travelling companion to Taoism and Buddhism the martial arts spread slowly across Asia, mixing or merging with the indigenous martial combat methods of other countries in the Orient.

The Shaolin temple

It is often disputed that, because such a wide variety of martial arts styles exists in China, they should all have had their place of origin at the Shaolin temple in Hunan. What is perhaps nearer to the truth is that there was a number of temples around the country where warrior monks trained in combat styles. The Shaolin monastery at the foot of the Song Shan mountains was probably the forerunner of later establishments elsewhere in the country, founded by priests who had qualified and gone out into the world. Because of this the various martial traditions were nurtured, underwent subtle changes and emerged as subdivisions of the major styles. Each style was named after the priest or monk who initiated the changes.

The original Shaolin temple was built around AD 495 by royal decree of the emperor Hsiao-Wen. Two hundred years later the first emperor of the T'ang dynasty, T'ai Tsung, appealed to the fighting monks for a force to help him defeat the usurper General Wang-Shih-Ch'ung who was aiming to establish a separate régime. The Shaolin monk soldiers aided their emperor and together they defeated Wang. Legend states that 13 monks gave their assistance, but in reality it was perhaps a much larger group, as the monastery was known to house at least 500 fighting monks. In recognition of their meritorious deeds the emperor conferred upon Shaolin the title 'Number One Monstery Under Heaven'.

In 1674 Shaolin was called upon yet again, to give assistance to its emperor and employ the monks' unique skills on the battlefield. They joined the Ch'ing emperor K'ang-Hsi in the conflict and defeated the enemy. After the war the fighting monks returned to Shaolin to resume their vocation in life. But this time they were to be poorly rewarded. Through petty jealousies

understand the rhythms of the universe that ruled the destiny of man.

Legend recalls that in the sixth century a certain Indian monk named Bodhidharma (in Chinese known as Ta-Mo or Da-Mo) crossed the Himalayas on foot and arrived at the Shaolin monastery in the Song Shan mountains of northern China. The purpose of his mission was to revitalize the Buddhist movement in China. Bodhidharma, finding the resident monks in a terrible physical condition, initiated a series of exercises based upon yoga breathing techniques. With their recovery Bodhidharma further instigated a regimen of physical conditioning, which was later documented on scrolls and became known as the I-chinching or muscle change classic. A martial art system developed from this, named Shih

SHAOLIN FISTS

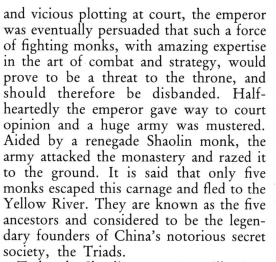

and vicious plotting at court, the emperor was eventually persuaded that such a force of fighting monks, with amazing expertise in the art of combat and strategy, would prove to be a threat to the throne, and should therefore be disbanded. Half-heartedly the emperor gave way to court opinion and a huge army was mustered. Aided by a renegade Shaolin monk, the army attacked the monastery and razed it to the ground. It is said that only five monks escaped this carnage and fled to the Yellow River. They are known as the five ancestors and considered to be the legendary founders of China's notorious secret society, the Triads.

Today the Shaolin monastery still exists, and attracts tourists from all over the world. It has been partly rebuilt by the Chinese People's Republic and is preserved as a historic monument.

The kung fu systems

Many kung fu styles have been based on the careful observations of animals fighting. An animal, having no interfering rational mind, moves freely and impulsively in an attack-and-defence situation. Therefore when undertaking the study of a martial system that is based on one particular animal, the underlying theme is to become like that animal, merging oneself through training to take on the nature of the beast. It is best explained as a kind of metamorphosis taking place, both mentally and physically, whereby the student completely identifies with the animal. So at any given moment an adept, if suddenly attacked, can quickly provide effective defence by employing the strength and ferocity of movement of say a tiger, or perhaps evade the counter-attack by adopting poses from the monkey style, imitating that animal's agility by leaping and rolling. The well-trained

2 *The attacker kicks to the groin area, but the defender quickly arches his body so the kick misses. At the same time he strikes downwards with an open palm, to prevent the kick from gathering full momentum.*

3 *The defender moves in quickly and counters with a back-fist strike to the nose. A cross-arm block prevents the attacker from throwing a punch with his left arm.*

Above This demonstration of the tiger claw stance is part of a strength and power form known as Kung-lik-kune. There are 167 moves in this intermediate form which is practised by students of Hap Kune-do, a system closely related to Hung Gar kung fu.

of mental and physical development, including speed and reflex training, together with the valuable psychological preparation for actual combative encounters, when faced with a real life-or-death situation.

The Chinese martial arts are usually separated into two distinct schools. The internal school comprises just three particular styles: they are tai chi chuan, pa-kua, and hsing-i. These 'soft' styles, as they are termed, use the concept of yielding to an attack rather than meeting it head on. They empitomize the Taoist principle of inaction, and take advantage of the opponent's committed attack by neutralizing it without exerting unnecessary energy. Thus the actual physical effort is minimized on the defender's part.

The second school consists of the external or 'hard' styles. These systems are associated with power strikes and hand and body conditioning. They utilize force in straight lines with emphasis on kicking techniques.

Tai chi chuan

Of the three internal styles of kung fu practised today, tai chi chuan has the greatest following. It has been adopted by the West more for its exercise principles than for its combat methods. The word translated means 'grand ultimate fist'. In effect it employs the Taoist practice of bringing positive and negative forces into harmony between the body and its surroundings through formalized exercises.

The tai chi 'form' is a continous slow-motion solo exercise whose primary objective is to teach practitioners how to attain spiritual and physical fitness, whereas the combat side of the art is secondary. The movements of tai chi are designed to allow the body to flow in a relaxed and smooth manner, without interruptions, and the structure of the form provides a method for calming the mind while concentrating at the awareness level. Because of its power to soothe, practice of tai chi is becoming more and more popular in the West for relieving stress at every level.

The combat side of tai chi embodies the principle of non-resistance to force, or 'yielding'. By yielding, the practitioner redirects the attack. Tai chi does not employ the blocks and strikes which are familiar in many other martial art forms. Movements are circular, so that an attack is taken around the circle and back into the aggressor. This requires a high degree of skill, and many years of training.

student's defensive movements are executed sharply and unconsciously, using pure reflex action.

Kung fu was developed to utilize efficiently the components of the human body for self-defence and also for valuable exercise to promote health. Training in one of the many kung fu styles consists of the systematic learning and practice of pre-arranged sets. Choreographed by the ancient masters to simulate various combative situations and their myriad combinations and possibilities, these pre-arranged movements guide the novice through a series of toughening-up exercises and stages

16

Even though tai chi is practised very slowly and the 128 movements of the solo exercise seem to be mesmeric in appearance, these movements are in fact dynamic in their structure, and are potentially very powerful. It is the ability of the practitioner to use the waist, to coordinate the whole body behind a movement, that gives it strength and thereby to acquire self-defence skills.

Because tai chi is the softest of the internal arts, the students of the hard styles of karate and kung fu seek it out to complement their own particular art. Many years are required to uncover the subtle secrets of tai chi. Once proper knowledge of the art is cultivated a practitioner will know how to ward off an on-coming attack and flow right into a counter-move. Warding off and counter-attacking are the key manoeuvres in tai chi, and for this reason it is said to reflect best of all the philosophical premises of yin and yang.

Origins

Legend relates that tai chi was founded by Chang San-Feng. Feng was a Taoist alchemist who lived in the mountains during the Yuan dynasty (1279-1368). After drinking a strange concoction one day, he fell into a deep sleep and had a dream in which he was taught a series of fighting manoeuvres all centring around completely yielding to an oncoming attack. He began to practise these each day and within two years his elderly frame began to grow strong and youthful. He believed that at last he had found the elixir of life.

Feng left the mountains to head for civilization and teach this new art to the people. In his journey through the wilderness it is said that on many occasions he was attacked by bandits who roamed the area. Feng defeated every one that came up against him.

In later life Chang Sen-Feng took a disciple under his wing named Chen Chia Kou and taught him everything about tai chi. The Chen family kept the secret of the form for over 400 years. Later on, Chen's descendants elaborated on the system and the style split into two branches. One member of the family was engaged by a druggist to teach his sons, and the servant of that family, Yang Lu-Chan, watched and learnt the style in secret until he was finally accepted as a student. Yang later went to Peking and taught the emperor's guards his 'internal' boxing methods. As a result the famous Yang tai chi form was developed which today is practised all over the world.

TAI CHI CHUAN

The following picture sequence shows the first half of one of the classic short forms of tai chi. The movements are always performed in a slow, relaxed and flowing manner so that each posture blends with the next.

1 *The feet are shoulder-width apart and the hands are raised and then lowered as if floating.*

2 ***Grasp sparrow's tail left and right***
When they reach waist level the weight is shifted to the right and the left hand dropped, palm up. The right hand is held in front of the chest, palm down. The two palms now face each other as if holding a large beach ball. A step is made on to the left foot and the left hand is raised. The right hand is lowered beside the right thigh. The eyes face front again.

The ball-like position is repeated to the right.

3 **Pull back** Then the right palm is raised while the left one is withdrawn a little. The trunk is moved backwards from the waist, spine straight. The right palm is turned out and the left one up. Meanwhile the weight is shifted on to the right foot.

4 **Press forward and push** The left palm is turned over and then pushes towards the right palm, without actually touching it. Both hands are then pushed out in front of the chest.

5 **Single whip** The weight is transferred first to the left foot while the right foot turns inwards, then back on to the right foot. As a turn is made the left hand drops and the two palms again form the ball shape. A step is taken on to the left foot and the left hand is raised to nose level. The right hand forms a 'hook' shape over the right toes.

6 **Raise hands** The left foot is turned in 45° from the heel and the waist moved to the right. The right heel touches the ground lightly. The right hand extends outwards at nose level, with the left level with the right elbow, palm in.

7 **Stork spreads its wings** The right hand is slanted down to the stomach as the weight is shifted on to the right foot. The waist is turned to the left while the left hand is moved downwards and the right up above the right ear.

8 **Left brush knee and twist** The right palm turns towards the face and is lowered. A step is made 45° to the left on to the left foot. At the same time the left hand guards the groin as if from a kick. Then a small step is taken to the right.

9   ***Play the fiddle*** The left hand is moved up until both are in the position shown in the photograph. Move 8 is repeated.

10   ***Step up, parry and punch*** With the weight on the right foot, an outward push is made with the left hand. *A loose right fist punches outwards, returning to waist level. After a step on to the left foot, the parry and punch is repeated, then the left hand brought inwards to the chest. The right hand punches and turns over, palm down.*

11   ***Apparent close-up*** The left palm moves under the right elbow, with the weight on the right foot. The hands swoop down and then up to the chest, palms out, the weight on the left foot.

    The hands rise, palms forward, the weight on the right foot, then the left, but with the trunk turning right.

12   ***Cross hands and carry tiger to mountain*** The hands circle out and down in front of the abdomen while the knees bend. The right hand guards the groin, the weight on the left foot. The waist turns to the right and a step back is taken 45° to the right, while the left hand pushes across the chest. Moves 3 and 4 are repeated.

13   ***Fist under elbow*** The weight moves on to the left foot while the right toes turn in. The ball shape is formed, the left palm below. The weight moves to the right foot, just behind the left. The hands reverse and as the waist turns left, a step is made with the right foot and a soft right fist is placed under the left elbow.

14   ***Step back and repulse monkey right and left*** A backward step is made with the left foot and the right fist opened and raised to the right ear, palm out. A slight push is made. The left palm faces up and is brought to the chest. The weight moves to the left leg and the right hand is lowered to the groin.

    The pushing move is repeated to the left.

15 **Step back and repulse monkey right** Look along the right arm and step back with the left leg. Push as before to the right, then bring the hand towards the chest. Turn the left palm up and shift the balance left. Meanwhile the right foot turns in.

16 **Slanting flying** Drop the right hand and form the ball shape. Turn the waist right and move the right foot back, heel first, till the weight is on the right foot. A slanting move is made with the hands, as in the left part of the picture.

17 **Cloud hands** The left foot is turned in from the heel and the left hand is circled downwards, clockwise, while the right circles in the opposite direction. Meanwhile the weight shifts left, then the right foot is brought near the left. The circles repeat and a step is made to the left. This is repeated four times.

18 **Golden cock stands on leg** After repeating move 5, the weight is shifted back and the knee bent, then transferred to the left foot. Meanwhile the left hand is dropped and the right raised. The balance is held. Repeat on the right leg.

19 **Separation right and left foot kick** Move back on the left leg, then again on the right. The right hand is raised to the ear then dropped and crossed in front of the left hand, the weight again on the left foot. A light kick is made with the right foot, aiming at an imaginary opponent's shin. The kick is repeated to the left, but both hands strike an imagined blow in each direction outwards.

20 **Turn and kick with sole** While balanced on the right foot, a turn is made 90° to the left and the hands are crossed in front of the chest, the right nearest the body. A kick is made with the sole and each hand again makes an imagined blow outwards.

The form continues with almost the same number of postures, finally ending in the same way in which it began.

Pa-kua

The second of the internal systems is pa-kua, sometimes referred to as the middle art because it forms a link between tai chi and hsing-i. Pa-kua translates as 'eight trigrams', which are the fundamental symbols of the *I-Ching* or the *Book of Changes*, reputed to be one of the oldest books in the world, dating back more than 3,000 years. The *I-Ching* has a dual role in Chinese thinking: it is an oracle or book of divination and also a manual of philosophical and moral doctrine. The book centres around the eight trigrams formalizing the interplay of yin and yang. These eight trigrams are combined into 64 hexagrams which are said to relate to the understanding of all things under heaven that are in nature.

In the practice of pa-kua the movements correspond with those original eight trigrams, and the emphasis is on turning in a circle with very few straight-line manoeuvres. Students begin by learning to 'walk the circle'; this is an exercise for gaining mastery of pa-kua's unique stepping patterns. As in tai chi which has the one form with 128 movements, so pa-kua has one central pattern which is the foundation on which the rest of the art is built. This is called Da Mu Hsing or Great Mother Form. Specific techniques are practised while walking this circle. The student's aim is to move around an opponent, constantly circling in an effort to find an opening in which to strike. This is the prime strategy. At later stages an internal energy is gradually developed, that of chi. This intrinsic power accumulates within the individual, and is perhaps one of the hardest qualities to understand, especially in the West where logic seems to rule and strength is identified with rippling muscles.

As the student develops his chi levels, the subtle body movements are totally relaxed. These involve spiralling and twisting. The spiralling is likened to a corkscrew, with the body spinning while moving up and down. The twisting is from the waist, with the aim of generating tremendous power. An exponent, when adept, can virtually turn his waist right around to its extremes, to promote a recoiling power that is quite exceptional.

The strikes in this art are all delivered with an open palm. These palm techniques are used in conjunction with the characteristic stepping movements. Although it may seem a contradiction in terms, pa-kua in its attack is actually defensive and evasive. The

Above *The sage-emperor Fu Hsi, who lived during the legendary period of pre-dynastic China. He is depicted with the tortoise whose shell supposedly inspired the invention of the eight trigrams, the symbolic pa-kua, seen to the left of the picture. These trigrams were used for divination purposes, as described in the I Ching. Fu Hsi was greatly revered; he wears the long nails of a scholar.*

21

priority is to blend with the opponent's attack rather than contend against it. The reasoning behind this is: When a person is attacked why should he or she stand there and either take it or try to block it, when all that is necessary is to move out of its way? Because there is no fixed stance in pa-kua, there is no need to stand rooted in one position. Fixed positions reduce manoeuvrability, whereas in pa-kua every movement and posture can be regarded as transitional.

Training in pa-kua, as indeed in all the nei-chia (internal systems), is a slow process. The many obstacles experienced come from within the practitioner. It is essential to eliminate the resistance of one's own body to the flow of movement. Performing in a relaxed and natural manner is often very difficult to someone who has to cope with life's day-to-day situations. Most beginners usually find that the harder they try to relax the more rigid they become. They find the movements uncomfortable, and in striving to make them more comfortable add tension to both mind and muscles, thereby defeating the purpose of the lesson and becoming frustrated. But, with perseverance, a state of calm and relaxation is eventually achieved. It is perhaps this initial problem of the slow and patient grounding in the art, that deters many martial artists from learning it. Added to this of course, is the lack of competent instructors. As in tai chi, pa-kua has no training drills and all practice is done solo.

History and origins

Comparatively speaking pa-kua is a newcomer to the martial arts, only coming to prominence in the last 200 years or so, although the concept of internal boxing goes back about 400 years or more. Pa-kua was brought to light mainly through the practices of its alleged founder Tung Hai-Chuan, who was a eunuch in the palace of the Ching emperor, Tao Kuang. Prior to this not a lot is known about the early life of Tung. He was a native of Hopei province, and he spent much of his time being one step in front of the law. During one brush with the authorities he escaped imprisonment by seeking refuge in a monastery, where he furthered his skills in Chinese boxing methods. But his constant bad behaviour and drunken ways led him to be expelled. After further adventures Tung headed for the mountains to become a bandit. It was here that he came upon an old Taoist hermit. He witnessed the remarkable sight of an aged man practising what appeared to be a boxing style, but nothing like the kung fu he himself had trained in, or for that matter had ever seen before. The old priest was twisting and spiralling up and down, walking backwards and forwards in a circle, constantly changing direction. The hermit executed these strange moves with all the grace and agility of a man 40 years his junior. Tung approached the monk for instruction in this mysterious art and spent the next 10 years perfecting his skills. Next we hear of Tung Hai-Chuan in Peking, where he was acknowledged by all for his genius in kung fu.

Many of Tung Hai-Chuan's miraculous feats have been recorded and handed down by way of myths and tales. One story describes Tung sleeping in a chair. A student, noticing him, crept up to throw a blanket over him. The blanket landed, but Tung had vanished and was found at the opposite end of the room in another chair and still asleep.

It is generally accepted that Tung is the founder of pa-kua, but many martial arts historians disagree and claim that pa-kua has its origins almost 5,000 years ago, around 2953-2838 BC when the emperor Fu Hsi first used the term. Fu Hsi is supposed to have gained his inspiration for these eight trigrams from the deeply scarred markings on the back of a tortoise's shell. The trigrams were linked, according to Fu Hsi, with the five elements of earth, metal, water, wood and fire, which through yin and yang constituted the creative force of the universe, or the Tao (way). The trigrams became incorporated into the *I-Ching*, as a means of foretelling the future.

Pa-kua, like the other internal styles, has been mainly influenced by Taoism, whereas the other Chinese systems of kung fu which were developed at Shaolin were mainly Buddhist.

One story relates how in AD 625, some Taoist martial arts masters and their students met some Shaolin masters and students and together formed a pa-kua style known as Numin. The head of this newly formed school was a master named Sun Fung Lee. Nu translated means a stream and min is the old Chinese word for people. It was quite literally a joining of two peoples into one particular stream of the martial arts.

In tai chi chuan there are the different styles such as Yang, Wu and Chen. In pa-kua, Numin is a style of the art; the art is the same, but with subtle, yet distinct differences as taught by various founding grandmasters.

The positioning of the hands is of great importance in this style of kung fu. In the picture to the right Master Chan shows a student the correct way to block a kick. There are eight basic palm positions (relating to the eight trigrams of the pa-kua), which in different combinations can produce 64 variations. The essence of Pa-kua is constant change and movements are always smooth and coordinated.

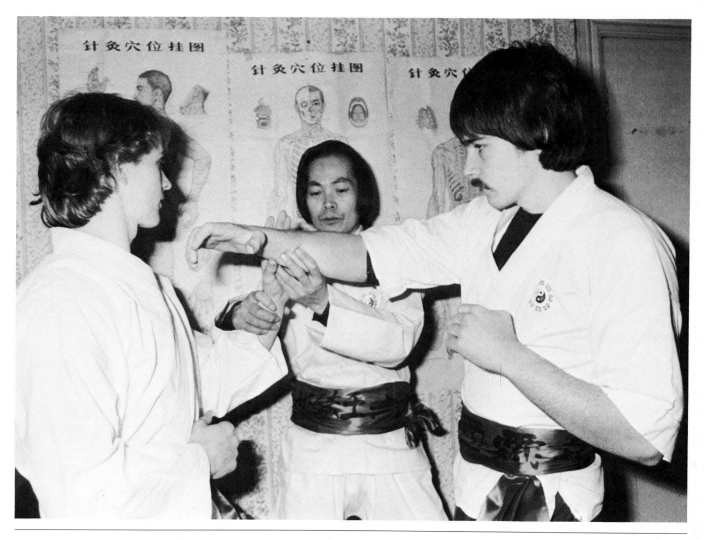

Hsing-i

The third art of the internal systems is that of hsing-i, but this is at the opposite end of the scale to tai chi. It is the hardest of the three, that is in application rather than degree of difficulty. In contrast to pa-kua, hsing-i places great emphasis on linear movement. It works on the geometric principle that the shortest distance to an object is along a straight line. This theory of the straight line is incorporated into the practitioner's belief that he should never retreat but continue advancing head on. The style is characterized by forceful horizontal attacks with closed-fist punches.

Hsing-i was created in the twelfth century by the Chinese warrior General Yueh Fei, and stresses the complementary principle of yin and yang, of both hard and soft. The term hsing-i is derived from two words, 'hsing' which means form, and 'i' the mind or will. Hsing-i is a physical manifestation of a philosophical premise. It reflects the Chinese belief that the yin and yang work through the five elements of wood, fire, water, earth and metal, each of which has the power to overcome another,

while being subject to the power of yet another. Take for example fire, which is overcome by water, whereas water is overcome by earth, earth by wood, and wood is conquered by metal which in turn is overcome by fire. The relationship between the martial arts and the theme of nature and the universe is constant.

In the art of hsing-i these elements are represented through the five basic movements, which are identified as splitting, crushing, pounding, drilling and crossing. Within this framework are the primary movements to cover all angles and direction of attack and defence. These basic motions have thousands of variations and are executed at very high speed. When the foundation of the five elements has been practised thoroughly, the student is then introduced to the first form called Lien Hwan Chuan, which links these separately practised movements into a definite pattern of connected sequences.

It is the aim of a hsing-i practitioner to unite the mind with the body, and this is perhaps why hsing-i is sometimes known as 'mind and body boxing'. There is very little wasted motion in the art; it is very direct in its application of short strikes. No tension is applied when punching, as the energy comes from within the body, rather than from muscular development. The physical techniques of hsing-i are not as important as the mental development; it is not so much a question of how much one does, but rather of how well one does it. Hsing-i stresses the development of chi energy, whose internal power is channelled to make the hsing-i student's body like a piece of steel.

Finally students are taught what is known as the 'twelve animals'. These are a series of short forms supposedly derived from the characteristics of certain animals, for example, the bird, snake, tiger, horse and dragon. Although students go through the process of learning these forms, it is usual to find that true technical competence is demonstrated in only two or three of them, depending on the student's own capabilities. This is probably due to the differing sizes and physiques of the individuals learning them. Each animal has its own potential for a system of fighting. It is not necessary to learn the whole twelve animals before one becomes adept. The most commonly taught form in hsing-i is that of the tiger.

CHI ENERGY

1 *Kung fu expert, Sifu Lam, prepares to demonstrate the astonishing power of his chi energy. He stands in the classic horse stance and five people push down on him with all their strength.*

2 *Sifu Lam applies his chi energy outwards and, with only a slight apparent movement of his arms, all five are repelled. (Notice the gap between his hands in pictures 1 and 2 – his only visible movement.)*

The mysterious energy named chi

No one can engage in the activities of the martial arts for too long without coming into contact with, or hearing about, a mysterious kind of apparently superhuman energy called chi. In karate and aikido it is known as ki and yogis refer to it as prana. This powerful unseen force lies within everyone and is capable of being tapped at any given moment by those who know how. The user can summon up abnormal amounts of strength and apply it instantly to given situations—anything from breaking a stack of roofing tiles with his bare hands to warding off an attack by two or more persons. Chi energy is cultivated in virtually every kung fu style practised today, and special emphasis is given to it in the internal styles.

To the ancient Chinese chi was the very substance that the universe was made of. The concept of a vital life energy permeated through the martial arts and into the realms of medicine, bringing into focus such healing skills as acupuncture and acupressure. As with everything Chinese the interplay of yin and yang is involved: what is good can also be evil. The dark side of the chi energy is that it can be used to kill, through a special technique known to few Chinese called dim mak or the death touch.

To the martial arts practitioner, the proper cultivation of chi power provides new heights of mental awareness, improved youthful vitality, good health and sharpened perceptions. All the Chinese martial arts emphasize the harmonizing of the body's internal power with the external techniques.

The correct terminology for the training of chi energy is called chi kung. The chi kung system is designed to develop the body internally by increasing the flow of the body's vital energy force. This is done via a series of breathing exercises and special movements. Unfortunately, chi cannot be seen to be developed, it is only felt and experienced. Because chi cannot be measured or analysed logically western science has for many years discounted its existence. However, with the recent success of acupuncture, which takes into account the chi energy flow and the correction of any imbalance to heal an illness, the medical world has begun to take seriously the ancient Chinese science of healing.

It is important to anyone beginning the chi kung exercises that they receive the correct instruction, as this powerful energy can harm as well as heal. The principal purpose of the exercises is to attain proper circulation of the blood, which in turn will ensure emotional stability. Correct breathing ensures that the blood is cleansed before feeding the vital organs of the body. Contrary to traditional western keep-fit exercises, the chi kung methods are practised without exertion or violent bodily movements. The ancient Chinese masters believed that if the internal organs were sound, anything was possible.

CHI KUNG

1 *Chi kung breathing exercises help to cleanse the organs and increase the vital energy flow around the body. After emptying the lungs, Sifu Austin Goh begins the exercises with double hands up, breathing in. After this, he opens his hands and breathes out.*

2 *He then crosses his palms and breathes in, after which the crossed palms are lowered and he breathes out again. The fists are clenched once more as he breathes in and opened as he breathes out, and clenched and raised as he breathes in again.*

3 *Flat palms are pushed forward with the outward breath. After this, the palms are pressed together in front, fingers pointing up, with the intake of breath.*

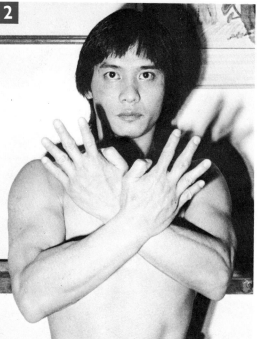

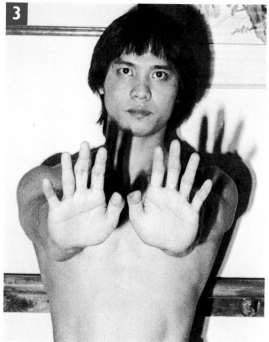

The iron palm

One branch of kung fu that utilizes the power of chi kung to the full is the Chinese art of iron palm. Before beginning the very exacting training, the master or instructor first has to treat each student with a special kind of secret liniment, known as the iron liquid. Every master has his own recipe, and only he himself knows the ingredients. Once treated with this, a student begins a set of exercises aimed at building up his chi power. After many months of these exercises the student learns to tap his chi energy source. He then trains on punching bags filled with dried beans. Within a year he transfers to bags filled with iron sand, practising to begin with for ten minutes or so each day, but gradually building up the length of time.

Once a student has begun iron palm training, a very strict regimen has to be maintained and great emphasis is placed on acquiring the correct amount of sleep. Every day he must train at a precise time; if he misses out he must start from scratch. The ancient masters say, 'Iron palm training is like a man paddling a boat up a river against the current. If he stops paddling even for a second, the boat doesn't stay still; it slips back. Then it takes him a long time to regain the position that he was in before he stopped paddling.'

Day by day, the bag training on the iron sand is practised and the iron palm medicine is applied. This goes on for two years and is then stopped. From then on the student trains with punches into thin air, rather like shadow boxing. At this point the chi energy begins to grow on a larger scale. The practitioner returns to the iron-sand bags only about once a month. The picture begins to emerge: the hard sand bags and the soft air, the yin and the yang, the positive and the negative, two opposites uniting to make a whole, the very essence of the Tao.

Once proficient in iron palm, an adept can kill a person without so much as marking the body, yet cause massive internal damage to the vital organs. In ancient China many a political figure from the emperor's court was mysteriously killed in this way. Nowadays iron palm is used to cure the sick and injured. This is achieved by the chi kung master generating his chi power and touching and vibrating various vital points on the body, to facilitate a recovery. In many cases the recovery is permanent. This touching is actually the master performing chi transference, using his powerful internal forces to unblock the chi energy channels of the sick people.

One hospital in London, England, has on file a record of a Chinese restaurant worker who after experiencing a severe blast in the face when an oven blew up, was left in agony with his face inflated like a football. Upon arrival at the hospital the injured Chinese, who incidentally was a master of tai chi chuan, was informed that his left eye was so badly injured he would probably lose the sight for ever. His right eye was also badly burned, and he was told that the vision could be impaired for years. As for his face, the doctors stated that he would need massive skin grafts.

It was time, the tai chi master thought, to put his chi energy into operation to initiate his own recovery. Within two weeks the sight in his right eye had returned. Over the next two months, through concentrated application of his chi energy to the eye the doctors had said would be blind for ever, the sight returned. New skin began to grow on his face with no apparent scarring. Six months later the master was completely healed, much to the total amazement of his western doctors.

The Pa Tuan Chin
Allied to chi kung exercises is a set form of a series of movements called the Pa Tuan Chin or Eight Section Brocade. These special health exercises are extremely popular on mainland China. Those western students who have taken the trouble to learn the movements have recorded that even after a few weeks' practice they no longer felt tired or listless in their everyday activities.

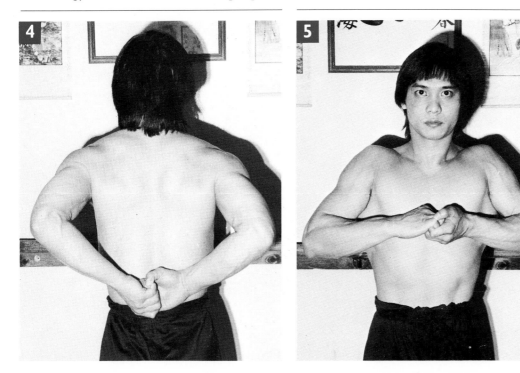

4 The exercises continue in similar fashion with palms together, fists clenched, then fingers jabbing forward, breathing regularly out and in and out. Then, as shown in this picture, he breathes in with a fireman's grip, then relaxes the hands down, fingers still joined, and breathes out.

5 Elbows are raised as he breathes in again. Then elbows are lowered to the outward breath, fingers joined. Two more moves complete the exercises, breathing in as the fists are raised to the shoulders, and breathing out as both palms push upwards to the sky.

THE POPULAR KUNG FU STYLES

'A teacher affects eternity: no one can tell where his
influence stops.'

During the twentieth century some of the movements that were once relevant to the various forms of Chinese boxing have been dropped, and new ones have been introduced that best suit the requirements of city dwellers in street survival situations. A few kung fu styles have needed only slight adjustments. In fact most of the ancient principles of unarmed combat are still as useful today as they were three and four hundred years ago in China.

Wing Chun

Without a doubt one of the most widespread and popular kung fu styles is that of Wing Chun. Wing Chun (also nicknamed Hong Kong street fighting) is a practical and scientific system of combat that cares little for the refinements of good taste. It is a lethal method of disposing of assailants, that is quick, sharp and to the point. Wing Chun has no superfluous techniques attached to it, nor does it embrace scores of different weapons. In fact there are only two types of weapon in the system, one being the luk-dim-boun kwan or six-and-a-half-point pole. The name comes from the number of movements that is the basis for all the techniques. The pole is about eight feet (2.4m) in length, although this can vary with the person using it. A Shaolin monk named Gee-Sin originated this art.

The other weapon of the system is the famous pak-charn dao or eight cutting knives, perhaps more familiarly known as the Wing Chun butterfly knives. The name derives from the use of the twin knives with their eight basic cutting movements.

The primary aims of Wing Chun are to guard the centre line of the body, and to exert only the minimum amount of force to do the maximum amount of work. Two-thirds of this style consists of hand manoeuvres and subtly shifting footwork. Very

Left A classical kung fu pose. The bent knees lower the centre of gravity and provide stability and are constantly used in the martial arts as a basis for sound defence and attack.

few kicks are employed at all, contrary to what the movies indicate. In actuality there are only eight kicks, all variable in execution. These kicks are short-range ones, and when they are delivered correctly they are almost undefendable. All the kicks except one are delivered low.

Wing Chun students first learn the basic hand techniques which act as both an attack and defence. The constant theme running throughout Wing Chun is that of economy of motion. This art is based on the theory that the shortest distance between two points is along a straight line.

To defend their centreline (an imaginary line running down the centre of the body, where the vital organs lie) students are taught never to present the enemy with a frontal target area, but to turn to the side. The hand techniques make use of the opponent's force to add momentum to the defender's counter-attack.

The overall simplicity of Wing Chun is evident by the number of forms or sets a student has to master in order to become proficient: there are only three. The first form is called Sil Lum Tao (little idea), the second form Chum Kui (searching for the bridge) and the last one is Bil Jee (stabbing fingers). During the time taken to learn these three forms the student also becomes conversant with a sparring exercise for two people, named chi sao or sticking hands. Chi sao heightens the student's sensitivity in the hands and arms to the point where it is possible to anticipate the opponent's intentions purely by the feel. This exercise also teaches mastery of elbow control and positioning. There are no set movements in chi sao; the aim is to attack from all angles and the opponent has to counter and re-direct his own attack.

After performing a good basic chi sao a student is blindfolded, because by now his reflexes and sensitivity will also be very

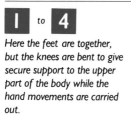

WING CHUN

The first two patterns that the student learns in Wing Chun kung fu both begin in a similar fashion, as shown in this sequence. The emphasis is on mastery of the complex hand movements, which must be properly coordinated with the breathing.

1 to **4** Here the feet are together, but the knees are bent to give secure support to the upper part of the body while the hand movements are carried out.

5 The toes are turned out as the fists are drawn in.

6 This is the main horse stance of Wing Chun style, in which the knees and feet are turned in

7 A crossed-wrists block protects the groin from a kick.

8 At a higher level a similar block prevents a blow to the face.

9 Open-hand moves are often followed by grabs or pulls.

10 The Wing Chun punch, in which the fist is thrust forward with a quick snapping action of the elbow.

11 This punch is aimed directly at the face. After impact, at full extension of the arm, the fist is quickly withdrawn by bending the elbow. The bottom three knuckles constitute the striking area.

12 to **14** Punches are often combined with grabs, pulls or pushes. One technique is never considered to be enough in Wing Chun style; it is always followed up by many more until the assailant is completely vanquished.

15 to **16** The form continues with emphasis on the centreline, the main line of defence and attack which runs vertically in front of the body.

good. This indicates that chi sao does not rely on the use of eyes, but more on the sensitivity developed, so that the student can feel his opponent's moves without actually seeing them.

The final part to learn in the system is the wooden dummy (mook jong). This is a special training device (though not unique to Wing Chun) which was built to resemble a human opponent. There are 108 traditional hand techniques which can be practised on the seven sections of the wooden dummy, although in later years these movements were increased to 116. This training device dates from the days of the Shaolin monastery. When the monks built their monasteries at Shaolin and Fukien, they set up a series of wooden men arranged in two straight rows, with a narrow passage going down the middle. Here the practitioner rehearsed his techniques while passing through. It was known as wooden dummy alley. In most Wing Chun kwoons (training places) the dummy is usually supported on a framework.

Left Wooden dummy training plays an important role in the development of Wing Chun hand techniques. Apart from speed and accuracy, it helps to harden the hands.

WING CHUN

Wing Chun exponents can attack and defend at the same time.

1 The knee is raised in preparation for a kick. The hands block, their position enabling them to grab immediately, or follow through with a strike from the left elbow.

2 The kick is delivered, using the heel as the striking area, a powerful weapon.

3 With the weight to the rear the front leg can be quickly lifted into a kick. The fingers of the right hand can be aimed at the eyes, while the left can block or grab.

4 A punch is delivered with the left fist while the right hand defends.

5 Although attacking with two hands, the front leg is always ready to defend.

6 The open hand is often used in Wing Chun style. Here it can be aimed at the neck or under the chin.

Right *This is the yang sao block in which a punch to the face can be deflected, then by quickly twisting the wrist and opening the hand a grab can be made, pulling the opponent on to a punch delivered by the right hand.*

Far right *The bong sao block is one of the three basic blocking positions. The elbow is flipped up to deflect a punch while the hand is ready to grab.*

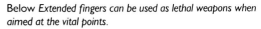
Below *Extended fingers can be used as lethal weapons when aimed at the vital points.*

Above *This two-handed block covers attacks to both the upper and lower areas of the body. By side-stepping, the defender borrows the opponent's strength.*

WING CHUN

 Several weapons prepare to strike at once, employing both hands and one leg.

2 A double punch and kick are delivered simultaneously. Wing Chun emphasizes multiple strikes.

The birth of Wing Chun

Wing Chun is particularly unusual in that it was actually invented by a woman, a Shaolin nun named Ng Mui. Ng Mui was one of the few people to escape the sacking of Shaolin by the Ching troops, when they burnt the monastery to the ground. She and a few of the monks managed to seek refuge in central China. Ng Mui was an instructor of mui fa chuan or plum flower fist. In the village where she settled down Ng Mui met a young girl named Yim Wing Chun, to whom she taught her system. But Yim Wing Chun thought that the plum flower fist was too complex and placed too much reliance on power techniques and strong horse stances, befitting a man rather than a woman. Yim Wing Chun wanted something that was not complicated yet efficient, as a means for defending herself. Not finding it among existing styles, she created her own. She dedicated her style to the Buddhist nun who had taught her, but named it after herself. Wing Chun means 'beautiful springtime'.

That was a little more than 400 years ago. The art first came to light in the West when its modern instigator, grandmaster Yip Man, known as the pioneer of Wing Chun, left the town of Fatshan on the Chinese mainland during the communist takeover to live in Hong Kong. Yip Man had one great desire, which was to make Wing Chun known all over the world. He achieved this aim in 1972, shortly before dying of throat cancer aged 78. These aims were largely due to the efforts of one of his most famous students, Bruce Lee.

3 A double finger jab again illustrates the use of more than one weapon at once. This is a side-on view of number 5 on the previous page.

4 Kicks are mostly low in this kung fu style. Here is a typical low kick executed with the heel. Notice how the fists continue to defend the centreline. The target of such a front kick (dim geak) would normally be the opponent's leg. Used a little higher, the target can be the groin or even the solar plexus.

5 Here the side of the foot is used as the weapon. This technique is often aimed at the opponent's supporting leg, to unbalance him.

35

Bruce Lee: a legend in his own time

Undoubtedly the man who had the largest influence on the martial arts in recent times was the late Bruce Lee, known to the Chinese people as 'the little dragon'. Bruce Lee's life story is by now fairly common knowledge. His early death at the height of his film career in 1973 stunned the world. The legacy he left behind was a fighting art *par excellence*, his Jeet Kune-do, translated as 'way of the intercepting fist'.

Bruce Lee was born in San Francisco in 1940, in the year of the dragon (by the Chinese calendar) of mixed parentage: a Chinese father and western mother. Within

a few months of his birth, his parents moved back to Hong Kong, where the young lad grew up. His interest in street fighting led him to begin training in the kung fu art of Wing Chun. His teacher was an older friend of his named William Cheung. A short time later William Cheung left for Australia, but before he went, he introduced Bruce to his own instructor, Yip Man. A certain amount of controversy surrounds Bruce's instruction with Yip Man. The reason was that at that time Yip Man was a very conservative Chinese, and strictly adhered to the un-

Above *Bruce Lee attained international stardom with his part in* Enter the Dragon. *This is a still from the film.*

36

written law that non-Chinese should not be taught the secrets of a kung fu system. Bruce Lee, not being of full Chinese blood, was taught virtually nothing by the grandmaster. So William Cheung arranged for Bruce to meet his fellow student Wong Sheung Leung, and it was from him that Bruce Lee learned the elementary principles of the Wing Chun system. When still only a young man Bruce Lee's fighting abilities were far in advance of his age and st... Over the following years Bruce be... formulate a fighting principle rather... system. He termed this principle j... Kune-do.

The intercepting fist strikes!

Bruce Lee abhorred the term 'style' as he thought this denoted a set way of teaching and learning, which was then passed on from instructor to student, down through the ages in exactly the same way, thus never creating any kind of individualism within the student. His belief was that everyone should tailor their fighting methods to suit themselves, rather than just imitating the instructor. His principle is to experiment with many styles and absorb from them whatever is useful for the individual's own size and build, eventually finishing up with a fresh type of freestyle.

Bruce Lee in his researches investigated every conceivable fighting system for this purpose, meanwhile developing and polishing his ideas into a modern and unorthodox combat system. Despite the fact that he proved his theories in actual contests, most instructors of the traditional systems degraded his ideas, labelling him a young upstart. Yet his skill and foresight in ...thods were actually light-years ... contemporaries.

...the jackpot in the world of ...erbly built body, honed to ...e ultimate fighting machine, struck the imaginations of the Hong Kong cinema audiences, and within a few short months he had hit the big-time. So great was this young actor's success, that the Hollywood bosses invited him to make a movie. The result was *Enter The Dragon*. This film brought him virtual overnight stardom when it received world-wide release, but this did not deter him from his quest for a perfect martial system.

His tragic early death from a brain edema, said to have been caused by hypersensitivity from taking an Equagesic headache tablet, deprived the martial arts world of a fighting genius whose full potential as a pathfinder into new realms of fighting concepts was never fully realized.

Below Bruce Lee's spectacular display of kung fu techniques in the Chinese-made Fists of Fury *helped to popularize Oriental martial arts in the West.*

Right *An unfriendly adversary feels the wrath of Bruce Lee during a scene from* Enter the Dragon.

Lee's philosophy

Even today, Bruce Lee's concept of Jeet Kune-do is still misunderstood. Jeet Kune-do is often thought of as a style, but it is not actually taught as a training method; it is an understanding. The student reaches this understanding through learning various martial arts. But it is not just a question of taking a technique from a particular style and putting it together with something else. One has to ask oneself: why does that technique work from that style? It is understanding the principle at the core that really counts. This principle can then be re-applied, once understood, to improve the student's own fighting ability.

The Jeet Kune-do philosophy is like any philosophy: people can give it their own interpretation. At times JKD (as it is known) has been termed contradictory by the traditionalists, because they have not fully comprehended what Bruce Lee was implying when he spoke those now famous words: 'Absorb what is useful, reject what is useless.' The idea of absorbing what is useful and rejecting what is useless is not just picking from different styles, thinking 'That's good, I like this' and putting the bits together. They are missing the concept, missing the real point. To absorb it, means to go into it, train in it (any particular martial art) become it, for a time. Once you have done this, that knowledge is then yours. Once you have grasped the essence then you can throw away whatever doesn't suit you personally. Looking for the essence is a hard route to follow. So the teaching has to be done on a one-to-one basis. The important thing about rejecting what is useless is that you don't reject until you know why. As Bruce Lee stated, 'When one has reached maturity in this art, one will have the formless form. It is like the dissolving of thawing ice into water, shaping itself to any structure. When one has no form, one can be all forms; when one has no style, one can fit in with any style.'

The Praying Mantis

Praying Mantis is a northern Sil Lum (Shaolin) style of kung fu. It is also known as Tanglang Chuan or Tong Long. A variation is Seven Stars Mantis, a style of fighting named after the Chinese theory of heavenly constellations, emphasizing continual movement and the changing of the angle of attack.

The initiator of this style was a martial arts fighter named Wong Long. It appears that after constantly being beaten in Chinese boxing matches with his fellow monks, despite his hard training, he finally retired to practise religious contemplation.

Below *The claw-like hands are typical of the style known as Severn Stars Praying Mantis.*

While sitting in a garden in a reflective mood, he observed two insects engaged in a fierce battle. The insects, one a praying mantis and the other a cicada which is a type of grasshopper, were locked in combat to the death. Wong Long's observations led him to realize that the mantis was fighting in a definite pattern, even though the cicada was much bigger and heavier. From its two front limbs the mantis made lightning strikes followed by quick withdrawals, attacking first to the left and then to the right in a vigorous manner. Among the insect's various striking methods, there were attacks from outstretched limbs as well as from limbs slightly retracted. These movements confused the cicada, which eventually flew off soundly defeated.

Wong Long caught a mantis and took it home with him. For days Wong Long played with the insect, prodding it with a blade of grass to analyse its reactions. He particularly noted that it could hook with its claw, in all directions. Wong Long then formulated a series of techniques based upon the mantis's mode of combat. Perfecting them over a number of years, he returned to the monastery ready to fight and beat every monk there. The abbot was immensely impressed, and the new art was named after the insect that had inspired it.

The techniques

The system employs two basic principles. The first is the grab. This is effected by shaping the hands to resemble that of a mantis's claw, with the index finger pointed forward. Grabbing is followed by pulling, to expose certain areas of the body. Then strikes are made to these vital points. Skilled pulling also ensures that the opponent is off balance. The second principle is what is known as 'monkey footwork', which does not, as the name implies, copy the footwork of a monkey, but rather imitates its speed and agility, while still giving support and balance. The stances are short, with a quick sideways stepping motion.

Although both northern and southern Mantis schools use the name of Praying Mantis in their titles, the methods and fighting principles of the styles are quite different. Northern Mantis stresses long-range fighting tactics and also includes a wide variety of kicks. Southern Mantis schools rely heavily upon in-fighting techniques delivered from close range with a more stable stance. Although kicks are seldom used, when they are, they are aimed at the groin or knee-caps.

Hung Gar kung fu

Right *The Chinese instructor or sifu walks up and down his kwoon during training, to ensure that his young students are in the correct stance—horse-riding stance—and are executing their punching techniques in the right way.*

Below right *Receiving a well-timed palm-heel strike under his chin, this attacker's punch misses its target.*

Legend has it that this style of kung fu was created when a master of the Tiger system, a monk named Hung, was tending the monastery vegetable garden. He noticed a crane pecking at his recently planted crops. In trying to shoo the bird away he found that no matter which way he struck, the crane eluded the blow. Then the crane would counter-attack, beating its wings down upon the monk and pecking him with its beak. This quite amazed the Tiger master, and so he undertook to commit every one of the bird's attacking movements to paper. He consequently incorporated his findings into his own fighting system. The crane and tiger system was named after him and became known as Hung Gar. Gar translates as family.

Hung Gar is characterized by internal power and low wide stances that produce strong solid legs. The movement in Hung Gar is direct and generally close to the body, but when a strike connects with an opponent, it can show considerable force. The strong low stance is also noticeable in other kung fu styles, but perhaps none emphasizes it as much as Hung Gar. This stance is called ma-pu or the horse stance.

The style's low stance reputedly came from Hung's secret training sessions on board Chinese junks (sailing vessels) while he was a rebel and on the run from the Manchus. These junks had very low roofs and bobbed about on the water constantly,

so therefore to practise successfully on a regular basis, it was necessary to adapt the Shaolin styles, with their sweeping foot patterns, to suit the confined space.

Because of the initial focus on this very low stance and the concentration on breathing exercises, more stamina and will power are required to learn the Hung Gar basics than those of other styles. In the early days of kung fu, students of Hung Gar were required to stand in the horse stance for as long as three hours at a time.

Hung Gar is a hard style that makes use of a blocking technique known as a pounding block, which is executed with a hammer fist. For a practitioner to apply this block meaningfully and correctly, he has to undergo a great deal of hand and arm conditioning.

Bok Hok Pai—the system of the White Crane

Bok Hok Pai, or White Crane, was invented by the Tibetan lamas. Originally the system was reserved solely for the use of hand-picked bodyguards to the emperor and empress of China. The secrecy of this style was preserved over the centuries until recent times when masters began to teach the art for a living.

A story relates that a lama was meditating on a hillside when he heard a commotion going on. Looking up, he saw a terrific fight going on between a white crane and a huge ape. The ape kept on charging at the crane, but the wily bird evaded the charges

and retaliated with its wings and claws. After a heated battle the ape turned and fled, blinded in one eye. The lama created eight different techniques based upon what he had witnessed. These used the natural movements of the white crane, but incorporated the ape's footwork and grabbing manoeuvres.

The art is now generally considered to be a long-range fighting style, and the system boasts ten sections covering weapons.

In the advanced stages of Bok Hok Pai students learn an 'internal' pattern (or kata) known as Cotton Needle Set. In the old days the traditional way to practise this was on mui fa joong (plum blossom poles). This entailed burying the ends of 14 ten-foot (3m) poles into the ground, about three feet (90cm) in depth, so that at least seven feet (2m) were protruding upwards. They were six inches (15cm) in diameter and placed about two feet (60cm) apart in the arrangement of a mui fa (plum blossom) design. Students would then climb the poles and once perched precariously on the top

41

would begin to execute the movements of the form.

Apparently some schools of Bok Hok Pai, as a test of true courage, used to place sharpened bamboo stakes in the ground beneath the poles, thus giving the students the added incentive of maintaining their balance at all costs! Today, thankfully, this practice is no longer in use, although in some schools a simulated mui fa joong is painted upon the kwoon (training place) floor.

Advanced students in kung fu will notice that White Crane techniques exist in many other systems, perhaps most noticeably in Hung Gar. But because of the internal aspects of Bok Hok Pai, to master the complete system can take a lifetime.

Choy Lee Fut

During the spread of kung fu techniques from the monasteries across China, many of the original styles were revised and modified, but it is not unusual to find striking similarities. An interesting and popular system is that of Choy Lee Fut, one of the most prevalent styles in Hong Kong today.

Chan Heung, the originator of the style, was born in King Mui village in Kwantung province *c.* 1802. From a very early age he was a student of Hung Gar kung fu. In his early twenties he decided to expand his knowledge of fighting styles, so he set out to search for a hermit named Choy Fook who lived somewhere in the mountains. This monk was famous throughout China as one of the greatest boxing masters of all time, but few people had been able to find him since his retirement. Chan Heung searched for many months until he eventually met up with him.

Chan Heung spent ten years with Choy, learning everything he could from his system. When Chan Heung was satisified that he had mastered sufficient techniques, he left Choy Fook and retired in solitude for a number of years to refine all that the monk had taught him. He added to this his Hung Gar experience and the few years' training he had had previously with another monk named Lee Yau-Shan. Then in 1836 Heung emerged with his own system, naming it after the two people who had given him the nucleus. The 'Fut', in Choy Lee Fut means Buddha in Chinese.

It was during this period that the Opium Wars broke out. Chan Heung joined a rebel militia, to use his kung fu skills fighting against the British. When China lost the war, which resulted in the signing of the Treaty of Nanking, Heung returned home deeply disappointed and bitter about the ambitions of the foreign carpetbaggers in his homeland. Over the following three years of 1847 to 1850, many secret societies began to spring up in the different provinces around Nanking. They fostered anti-British feelings, which eventually led to a revolt which was quickly quashed by the Chinese imperial troops. Chan Heung was asked to join the rebel army against the imperial troops, but being a devout Buddhist, did not like the idea of fighting his own kind. So he and his family left home. In the many places he travelled he instructed followers in Choy Lee Fut, establishing training schools in many parts of China.

Chang Heung died in 1875, with the knowledge that his style would be perpetuated, thanks to his many students.

The system applied

The characteristics of Choy Lee Fut are movements generally involving long stretches of the arms. This system has many forms or patterns: 29 to be precise. The names of some of these forms echo the style's roots, which reach way back to the Shaolin temple, such as the Eighteen Buddhas' Form. There are five basic stances which are termed the 'five wheel stances'.

Right The kung fu style of Choi Lee Fut uses a noticeably lower and wider stance than other kung fu systems, and the punch employs a longer arm.

These are noticeably different from other forms of kung fu, such as Wing Chun, because they are much lower, and are characteristically wide and powerful. Beginners are required to learn the basic stances and practise them thoroughly, before being allowed to advance, with the belief that people who progress too speedily can retrogress sharply.

Many weapons are used in the style such as the tiger fork and double knives. Perhaps the most unusual is the 'nine dragon trident'. The head of this spear type of weapon has nine objects resembling hooks, thought to remind users of dragons' teeth. This weapon is so heavy that ordinary practitioners have trouble using it.

The wu shu of mainland China

Many people in the western world suppose that kung fu is practised by a minority. In real terms the people of mainland China train every day in one form of martial art or another. The Chinese Communist government was quick to realize the importance of a fit and healthy nation, so the old war arts of China were revamped and keenly encouraged.

Wu shu means war arts, although the way they are practised today has little relevance to their original aims. Wu shu embraces as many as 200 different styles of kung fu and is used purely as a generic term. The wu shu of the People's Republic is highly gymnastic, an art form which is also very much geared towards the sporting element. Children learn the arts from very early years in special athletics schools and display outstanding grace and agility in their performances. It has been calculated that over 50 million Chinese on the mainland are training in some form of wu shu.

The Chinese government, having heard how enthusiastic the western nations were about the practice of kung fu, sent out delegations supported by the All China National Sport Service, to put on demonstrations and exhibitions, so that westerners would have a chance to see the more obscure kung fu styles.

Fantastic weapons

The arsenal of the wu shu adept is truly amazing. Weapons from long ago are used with a technical competence that is quite outstanding. Children aged seven and eight years display wonderful forms utilizing such archaic weapons as the nine-section whip, long tassell sword, iron fan, sword and shield, and three-sectioned staff. The list is endless; it would appear that we in the West have barely scratched the surface of what actually exists in the world of kung fu.

One aspect of wu shu that seems to gain attention is yingqigong or 'training for the vital air', which in essence is chi energy training. In demonstrations, the wu shu troupes have placed sharp spear points at the throats of yingqigong experts, pushing the spears with considerable force. But never once have the spears managed to pierce the skin. On other occasions huge blocks of concrete have been placed upon the exponent's chest and then smashed by someone wielding a large hammer, but the yingqigong expert is never injured. The explanation is that the vital air is directed towards the spot in the body where the action is. This strengthens the area and makes it able to withstand any amount of punishment. Western audiences have witnessed many scenes such as these with disbelief. Such is the power of the kung fu practitioner.

Below *Students of the Hopei District Amateur Athletic School in Tientsin fence with spear and broadsword.*

The Mischievous Monkey

An unusual style of kung fu is that of the Mischievous Monkey, or, to give it its correct title, Ta Sheng Pi Kua Mern. The system is in fact two styles combined.

Ta sheng was founded by Kou Sze during the early years of the Chinese Republic (1911-1949). He was already proficient in an obscure style of kung fu called Ti Tang Mern or Grand Earth Method, which specialized in ground fighting techniques and kicks. Kou Sze worked as a bodyguard, but because of the trouble and turmoil in the new republic, he planned to give up his job and return home. On the way, while staying in a little village, he was arrested and accused of murdering another man during a fight. Kou Sze explained to the authorities that the death had occurred purely as a result of defending himself. Four men had attacked him as he was passing through the town. He had beaten them off using his kung fu skills, but unfortunately one of them had died. He was believed and on these grounds spared the death penalty, but sentenced to eight years' imprisonment.

His cell window faced a hillside on which resided a colony of monkeys. Every day while practising his kung fu in the confines of his cell, he watched the monkeys playing and fighting. Kou Sze became fascinated by their speed and agility and in the way they seemed to make very crafty moves. By observing them closely he began to catalogue their many and varied movements. Later he adapted these monkey antics into his own training regimen. By the end of his sentence, Kou Sze had perfected his new style.

Upon leaving prison Kou Sze went to see his friend who was a master of Pi Kua Mern, but found he had died. The son offered to put him up for a time. Kou Sze told his friend's son about his new style and explained that he had named it Ta Sheng (great sage) in honour of the monkey king god. The son was impressed and took it upon himself to learn the complete system from Kou Sze.

When Kou Sze died some years later, the son merged his own style of Pi Kua Mern with the monkey style, to form one system called Ta Sheng Pi Kua Mern.

Technique

The expanded Monkey style consists of five sets or forms called Lost Monkey, Tall Monkey, Stone Monkey, Wooden Monkey and Drunken Monkey. From these sets a student learns to react instantly to varied situations using long-range fighting techniques. He develops power and body toughening. Emphasis is placed on unpredictability and deception in attacking.

The last form, that of the Drunken Monkey, is perhaps the most famous. This set is supposedly based upon the actions of a monkey that stole some wine and subsequently became drunk. The fighting techniques accredited to this form teach the student to stagger and lurch around as if drunk. This ploy baffles the opponent, sometimes amusing him, so the exponent catches his aggressor off guard and suddenly launches into a series of strong unsuspected attacks.

A student of this style has to adopt the mannerisms and behaviour of a monkey, truly to understand the principle behind the art. It is not uncommon to enter a kwoon and see students pulling faces, screeching, and jumping up and down, in effect becoming monkeys.

Today the style's head is grandmaster Chan Sau Chung whose headquarters are in Kowloon Hong Kong.

The Oriental viewpoint

We have seen that in the Chinese martial arts, everything seems to revolve around religion and medicine as well as fighting. Throughout the East the relationship between these three is always close. In fact had it not been for the monks and priests, perhaps the martial arts as we have come to know them today would not be as widespread.

To the western mind fighting and medicine are at different ends of the scale, with religion even farther removed. Western students enter into the Eastern martial disciplines and find themselves faced with a mental attitude alien to their own. It is no wonder that many give up their training after a few short months. To accept in a short space of time Asian ideals, thoughts and disciplines, which have evolved over thousands of years, can seem quite daunting. Yet the few individuals who stay on to see their training bear fruition, realize that it is well worth all the time and effort spent. They are not just learning a sport, but a whole new way of life.

Everything done in this day and age is done in a hurry. The martial arts have developed over hundreds of years. To attempt short cuts only leads to cheating oneself of the true meaning and essence of what the martial arts are really all about.

KARATE— OKINAWAN HAND

'He who wishes to know the road through the mountains must ask those who have already trodden it.'

If it were not for the fact that Asia's feudal systems had lasted longer than those of other continents, the martial arts would almost certainly have died out or perhaps remained in the cultural heritage in the form of folk dances. Fortunately they did survive and their inherent values have become appreciated by people no longer at war, in all parts of the world.

The trading routes of the far East in ancient times were much travelled. Even though countries were many thousands of miles apart, a vast band of sailors, monks in search of truth and knowledge, traders with caravans of goods, all plied their wares and voiced their philosophies on their great journeys. Cultures exchanged with one another ideas on art and religion. This way much of Asia's development in different areas became interwoven. Most important-ly for the martial arts, the fighting skills of kung fu spread from China, via Okinawa, to Japan.

Okinawa, the birthplace of karate

The Ryukyus are an island chain mid-way between Japan and China. The largest of these islands is Okinawa. It is here that karate was born, although at that time it was known as Okinawa-te, or Okinawan hand. The influence of China's martial systems had penetrated Okinawa through the continued visits of various delegations and traders. Buddhist monks also found their way to this island kingdom. Over the centuries Okinawa had seen much intervention from Japan and the native Okinawans were inevitably caught up with political intrigue. Then in 1609 Japan laun-ched a large-scale invasion and completely overran the island. They quickly set up a seat of government in the island's capital of Naha, and the first edict they issued was a complete ban on the carrying of all weapons by islanders.

An area known as the Nine Villages was the authorized place of residence for the Chinese missionaries. Some of the islanders persuaded members of these missions to instruct them in their martial arts, and over the ensuing years the Okinawans blended the Chinese styles with their own indige-nous fighting systems.

Three main schools of fighting came into being, known as Naha-te, Tomari-te and Shuri-te. These names indicated the par-ticular town where each one had been nurtured. Great masters began to emerge, instilling into the people a new sense of hope. Stories began to circulate about masters who could pound trees every day in the forest with their fists, until the trees died. Others were said to be able to punch the ground and with one blow bury their fist up to the elbow. The exploits of the island rebels who had banded together to rid their land of the Japanese tyrants were quite incredible. They could ambush a mounted Japanese warrior, and unseat him with a flying sidekick. The heel of the rebel would have been hardened to such an extend it could penetrate the loose leather armour worn by the enemy and strike at a vital point to kill him.

Fight as they did, the Okinawans had to resign themselves to the fact that their Japanese overlords would be with them for ever. As history shows, Okinawa eventual-ly became merged with Japan in both culture and government.

Fighting skills such as the native Okina-wans possesed, did not go unnoticed by the Japanese. Being a warrior race themselves, the Japanese investigated this unarmed method of killing. During a visit by the Japanese navy to the island, a schoolmaster by the name of Gichin Funakoshi was persuaded to put on a martial arts demon-stration. The navy's impressions of what they saw were reported back to Japan.

Left Sensei Kanazawa, one of the foremost exponents of Shotokan karate, demonstrating kata.

KARATE KUMITE

Throughout the early grades of karate training, sparring (kumite) is formalized into set movements. Thus students can learn the techniques in controlled conditions without coming to harm or running the risk of hurting their opponents. The following sequences are from the Shotokan style.

1 *The formalized sparring always begins with a bow as a mark of respect to the opponent.*

2 *Then the attacker performs a downward block (gedan-barai).*

News reached the emperor of this deadly martial art and Gichin Funakoshi was invited to Japan to put a display on for the emperor himself.

Okinawa-te caused an uproar in Japan. Everyone seemed to want to know more about it. Gichin Funakoshi eventually settled in Japan and opened up a school, which he named Shotokan, or the club of Shoto. 'Kan' means hall and the name Shoto was Funakoshi's pen-name from the days when he used to write poetry; it means waving pines.

The emergence of karate

Until Funakoshi settled in Japan karate was still known as Okinawan hand. It wasn't until later that it was changed into Japanese characters to read karate-do or way of the empty hand. Although Funakoshi's style was of Shuri-te origin, taught to him by a great master named Azato, once in Japan he began to make subtle modifications to the system. To Funakoshi karate was not just a martial art, but it was also a way of building character in individuals.

In the years following Funakoshi's arrival in Japan, several other styles developed, some of which were introduced by other Okinawan masters following in his footsteps. Each style had its own techniques and predilections. Karate began to grow in popularity and by the 1930s all the major universities had thriving clubs.

Funakoshi's son, Yoshitaka, was becoming a driving force behind his father's style. The now famous karate round-house kick (mawashi-geri) is accredited to Yoshitaka. By 1936 Gichin Funakoshi had established his main dojo (training place) in Tokyo and his son began to introduce many new ideas, until gradually the art lost some of its distinctive Okinawan features.

Intense rivalry grew up among the students of different styles. Additionally, former students were now becoming instructors in their own right with their own individual ways, and karate began to fragment.

During World War II karate was taught to the Japanese imperial army. When the American occupation forces took over in 1945, General MacArthur banned it for a time. During this period Yoshitaka Funakoshi died of starvation after refusing American rations. He has been described as the greatest genius in the history of karate.

In 1955 the Japanese Karate Association was formed; then in April 1957 Gichin Funakoshi, whom many have termed the father of karate, died aged 88 years. In the late 50s karate reached Europe through the efforts of a French martial arts enthusiast named Henri Plée, and has subsequently spread across the world. Many countries have at least one resident Japanese karate instructor.

The styles

Modern karate is based almost entirely on strikes, using high-impact kicks and punches. The techniques are applied in various ways depending on the style followed. The emphasis upon what is important and what is not, also differs. For instance, in many of the Okinawan systems competition is looked down on, with the belief that karate was developed purely for self-defence, a highly dangerous art easily capable of killing with one blow. Japanese systems on the other hand have developed sporting aspects to the art, and competitions now take place at world level. Indeed, hope is high that soon karate will gain a place in the Olympic Games.

The styles of karate are not as distinct as those of kung fu. Many of them at first sight look reasonably similar to one

THREE-ATTACK SPARRING

1 The attacker (here on the right) steps forward three times with a front punch. Each time the defender blocks and steps back.

2 After the last block, the defender counterattacks with a reverse punch to the stomach.

ONE-ATTACK SPARRING

Students then move on to one-attack sparring when defenders can counter in various ways, thus building up a repertoire of moves.

1 After the downward block, the attacker calls out 'chudan', and steps forward with a punch to the stomach. The defender steps back slightly and seizes the attacking arm pulling the attacker on to a front kick (mae-geri).

2 He then steps forward and follows up with an elbow strike (empi) under the chin.

ONE-ATTACK SPARRING

1 *Another example of one-attack sparring, in which the defender steps into back stance and blocks with a knife hand (shuto-uke).*

2 *He then counters with a ridge-hand strike (haito) to the neck. In this technique the thumb side of the knife hand is employed, with the thumb moved inwards as far as possible. The impact area, the base of the index finger, is thus exposed for the strike.*

Below *Serious students of karate practise punching on the makiwara. This device hardens the fist, eventually building up callouses. It also gives the student the feel of making proper contact with a punch.*

ONE-ATTACK SPARRING

1 In this example, the attacker again punches to the stomach. The defender steps to the side and blocks.

2 Then the defender grabs the attacker's arm and makes a reverse roundhouse kick (ura-mawashi) to the head.

3 He uses the same leg to sweep away the attacker's front foot, who then falls to the floor.

4 The defender follows up with a finishing punch to the head and 'kiai'.

51

another, although Gojuryu karate, for instance, has more obvious differences. It is generally accepted that the style with the greatest following in the world is that of shotokan.

Shotokan

This style of karate, founded by Gichin Funakoshi, is characterized by deep stances and powerful extended movements. It has numerous kata (forms) which are practised with maximum strength. Funakoshi regarded the kata as the ultimate expression of his art, and devised many of them himself. The style uses considerable muscle power in the delivery of its techniques, which are linear in their application.

Of the many great Shotokan stylists Hirokazu Kanazawa stands out as perhaps one of the most skilful fighters of all time. In 1957 at the first All Japan Karate Championships he won every fight, including the final, with a broken hand—usually delivering the decisive blow with that hand. He accomplished this without ever having formally trained in free sparring for competition. The following year he won the championships again, only this time he also took the kata section. In recent years Kanazawa began a serious study of tai chi chuan, to improve his health and extend his knowledge of the internal systems of the martial arts.

SEMI-FREESTYLE

Advanced students practise semi-freestyle fighting before moving on to competition freestyle.

 The stance is slightly higher than in basic techniques and the fists are held in fighting position.

 The attacker's kick to the stomach is blocked with gedan-barai.

3 *This is followed up with a swift roundhouse kick (mawashi-geri) to the head.*

Kyokushinkai

This style was created by Masatatsu Oyama, who was once a student of Shotokan under Funakoshi. Oyama was born in Korea, and was influenced by Chinese and Korean martial arts before he trained in Shotokan. Not particularly impressed with the combat side of Funakoshi's style, he retired to the mountains in Chiba, where for the next two years he lived the life of a recluse. During this self-inflicted isolation, through intensive training and searching he formulated a new karate system that was based upon actual combat effectiveness. He named this new style Kyokushinkai or 'style of the ultimate truth'. To prove how realistic his new concept was, Oyama went to a slaughter house to fight with bulls. It has been recorded that over a period of time he fought 50 bulls, killing three of them outright with combination striking techniques.

In the early 1970s Oyama introduced a type of competition called knockdown. He has stated that this is the only true test of a karateka's fighting ability. It allows full-power strikes to the body and kicks to the head. The bout ends when one of the fighters is knocked to the ground. Kyokushinkai training is severe and requires a certain amount of conditioning. It has been classed as one of the toughest styles there is. Oyama has never stuck rigidly to the traditional techniques of karate, and is known to have looked outside his own martial art for superior methods.

Right Although full contact is made in kyokushinkai tournaments, competitors are allowed no protective equipment apart from shin protectors and groin guards.

Wado-ryu

Wado-ryu was created by Hidenori Otsuka, and its name means way of peace or harmony. Otsuka was another of Gichin Funakoshi's senior students. He was born in 1892 and his childhood was spent in the study of Shindo Yoshin Ryu jiu-jitsu. He became so accomplished in this art he was awarded the headmastership of the style.

He first began the study of karate at 30 years of age under Funakoshi. Ten years later he broke away to form his own style, but for a number of years it had no name. Then in 1940, at a martial arts festival, he was asked to register a name for his school, which he did, calling it Wado.

Hidenori Otsuka drew heavily upon his knowledge of jiu-jitsu and merged it with his karate, to found his style. This amalgamation of the yielding principles of jiu-jitsu, the non-opposition to strength, with the traditional Okinawan karate techniques gave a softness to the style that is unique in Japanese karate. Otsuka's karate system has a tremendously fast style and it is thought by many to be the fastest of all. Otsuka taught that the physical techniques and movements within Wado are the expression of one's mind, in fact a manifestation of a person's spirit. He acknowledged three vital elements in the study of karate: physical strength, spirit and heart.

As Otsuka's system developed he felt that the art should embrace an element of sport. To this end he invented kumite (sparring). Prior to this, there was no fighting in Wado, just kata training. After World War II his style spread into Europe and America.

He was awarded his tenth dan (black belt ranking) by the brother of the emperor of Japan, and he subsequently became the oldest practising karateka in the world. Then on the 29 January 1982, just four months short of his 90th birthday, Hidenori Otsuka passed away.

The practice of Wado-ryu karate employs very light and fast techniques, favouring evasion, rather than meeting brute force head on. The practitioner defends by using a series of deflecting movements for blocking, then quickly counterattacks as soon as the opening occurs. Twisting of the hips for increased power is also emphasized in this style. The basic stance is higher than it is in Shotokan, thus enhancing speed and mobility. Students are taught to punch by creating a very fast type of whiplash movement. After delivery of a technique, the hand or foot is snapped back

sharply to avoid capture by the opponent.

Because the style is competition orientated, a large amount of success has been accorded to its tournament practitioners in the world arena. In the late 70s Wado-ryu in Europe splintered into a number of different associations, but undoubtedly its leading instructor is Tatsuo Suzuki, eighth dan, who resides in London.

Shito-ryu

Shito-ryu karate was created by Kenwa Mabuni, an Okinawan. He had studied under the same master as Funakoshi. Mabuni had two teachers, Itosu and Higaonna, and it is after these two instructors that Mabuni named his style. The word comes from the Japanese characters used to write his teachers' names. Following in Funakoshi's footsteps, Mabuni began teaching karate in Japan, opening his first club in Osaka in 1934. Mabuni had a particular penchant for the practice of kata, and began to assimilate as many as possible, taking katas from the schools of Shotokan, Goju, and Shorin-ryu. In all there are more than 60 different katas, including those employing weapons.

One of Mabuni's senior students, Chojiro Tani, split from the association to develop his own theories on karate aimed at tournament fighting, which was becoming increasingly popular. Chojiro Tani named his new style Shukokai.

Above In this major inner reaping throw, Sensei Suzuki pushes down his opponent's right shoulder, while lifting his leg. This creates a see-saw effect, forcing the opponent on to the ground.

WADO-RYU KARATE

1 *Sensei Suzuki is confronted by Sensei Sugasawa. Both demonstrate ma-ai (distance) and zanshin (awareness).*

2 *To stop any front punch from Sugasawa, Suzuki shifts his weight to his right leg and covers Sugasawa's right hand.*

3 *Suzuki quickly steps around to trap Sugasawa's right leg and unbalance him, simultaneously applying a sharp knife-hand strike (shuto-uke) to the biceps to numb the arm.*

4 *Rotation of the hips provides impetus to the elbow attack (empi) to the face. This is a strong and highly effective short-range technique.*

Shukokai karate

Thus, Shukokai became the modern version of Tani's style of Shito-ryu. The translation means 'way for all'. Tani's innovative research and experimentation led to higher stances, faster kicks and direct blocks. The style was developed for speed and, because of the shorter stances, promoted good mobility. The delivery of attack appears to take importance over everything else. Shukokai teaches relaxation before the impact of a punch, thereby increasing acceleration and creating a greater force. It was to this end that foam punching pads were introduced as training aids. The student can hit the pad which is held by the training partner and actually feel the power he is generating, rather than spend weeks punching into thin air.

Tani's original style was rather limited, especially as far as the kicks were concerned. Combination techniques were practically unheard of. The early Shukokai practitioner believed wholeheartedly in the one-blow punch, and would never put two or three together; the idea was that if you needed three punches, then you were not putting everything into the first one. Later on, however, the style became influenced by the West, where practitioners wanted to be entertained as well as taught so—for sporting reasons—the number of kicks and punches were expanded and combinations became the order of the day.

The basic stance in the style is simply that of a person walking. The mechanical movements practised in some of the other karate schools in Japan were strictly discouraged, the emphasis being placed on naturalness and relaxed use of the limbs. The system emphasizes open-hand techniques to avoid tension; the reasoning behind this is that if students clench their fists they will instinctively want to squeeze, thus tightening their muscles. The open hand also allows a very flexible wrist action, giving increased acceleration for punching or blocking.

The system split again in later years when one of Tani's students did exactly the same that he had done, and left the school to found his own system. His name was Yoshinao Nanbu.

Sankukai karate

Sankukai karate was therefore developed from Shukokai by Yoshinao Nanbu. Nanbu had been a very successful tournament fighter, having won the All Japan Student Karate Championships three times. For some reason he became disillusioned with Shukokai and drifted in and out of other

BAG TRAINING

Many styles of karate emphasize training with a punch bag, so that the practitioner can gauge his own power and feel the impact of the techniques.

 Here a reverse knife-hand strike is the technique practised.

 Application of the knee can create a disabling blow and is considered a valuable technique in street self-defence situations.

styles to see what else they had to offer, but found nothing that appealed to him. He disappeared for a time, only to emerge a few years later with his own style called Sankukai. Although not one of the biggest organizations in the karate world, it did attract a number of followers. The style has a marked resemblance to some Chinese systems, but bears the typically Japanese stamp.

Some years later disillusionment set in again and Nanbu left his own organization once more in search of something different. His present style is that of Nanbudo or 'the way of Nanbu'. It is quite far removed from the Japanese systems, more obviously affiliated to the traditional kung fu of China. Nanbudo karate places a certain amount of stress on a health exercise of Chinese origins called Nanbu Taiso.

Shotokai karate

This style of karate is similar to Shotokan in that the stances are low. This is not surprising as Shotokai broke away from Shotokan due to the belief that Shotokan was deviating from its traditional teachings as laid down by Gichin Funakoshi. This split was led by many of the older instructors, who did not see eye to eye with the more modern exponents. The instigator of this breakaway movement was Egami sensei (master Egami).

Goju-ryu

Goju-ryu, which means hard-soft style, was created by an Okinawan named Chojun Miyagi. Goju is one of the four major karate styles developed from the Okinawan art of Naha-te. It is based on the yin and yang principles of soft and hard.

Chojun Miyagi began training in Naha-te at the age of 14 under the renowned instructor Kanryo Higaonna. As a youth Higaonna had made several trips to mainland China, while working for a trading company. For a time he stayed on in China to learn Chinese boxing. Upon his return he merged his ideas with those of the indigenous karate systems of Okinawa. Two of his top students were Chojun Miyagi and Kenwa Mabuni.

After his master's death, Miyagi decided that he too would journey to the Chinese mainland to continue his studies. While there, Miyagi was greatly influenced by the subtleties of the Chinese internal systems of kung fu. Returning home to Okinawa a few years later he quickly established him-

Below *Sensei Yamaguchi, son of The Cat, does a private work-out at his club in San Francisco. Here he performs an empi (elbow attack).*

self as a karate teacher *par excellence*.

Following the introduction of Funakoshi's karate to Japan, Okinawan teachers were in great demand. In 1928 Miyagi accepted a position as karate instructor at Kyoto university, but Japan never really appealed to him. After bouts of homesickness he returned to Okinawa, only visiting Japan for limited periods.

Chojun Miyagi devoted his whole life to the furtherance of Goju karate. He died on 8 October 1953 aged 65. During his lifetime, he saw his style remain pure, following the traditional patterns he had formulated, unlike other karate styles which were splintering. While Miyagi was in Japan, he taught a student named Gogen Yamaguchi. This student was to make a name for himself as the head of an off-shoot of Goju, called Goju-kai.

Goju-kai

When Chojun Miyagi modified his Goju, after a visit to Shanghai to examine more of the Chinese systems, a one-time student of his, Gogen Yamaguchi, refused to accept the adjustments, believing that the old ways were the best. Thus, he broke away to form his own style called Goju-kai. Yamaguchi, known in karate circles throughout the world as The Cat, developed Goju in Japan until it received the recognition that it has today. Because Miyagi refused to stay for long periods at a time in Japan, it was left to Yamaguchi to popularize his own system.

When Yamaguchi realized just how important he had become in Japanese karate circles, he took on his responsibilities in earnest. For a time he went into the mountains to seek spiritual guidance from a group of Shinto priests. Once a wild-man of karate, he now began a hard training regimen, and would meditate for long periods, going without food or drink, sometimes standing for hours under icy cold mountain waterfalls in the classical stance of goju sanchin (hourglass stance).

During World War II he was captured by the Russians and shipped off to a labour camp in Mongolia. It was here, despite terrible hardship and deprivation, that

Yamaguchi's karate spirit enabled him to survive. Nearly a year later he was repatriated, and in 1948 he opened his first dojo in Japan. Two years later he established the All Japan Karate-do Goju-Kai.

The techniques in Goju centre around close-quarter fighting. This highly complex style is quite exacting, requiring a balance between hard and soft, with the ability to change techniques in a quickly flowing, yet strong manner. The traditions of the school are maintained through training methods which are not just based on muscular strength; a great deal of emphasis is placed upon special breathing techniques. A be-

GOJU-RYU KARATE

1 *Power training is part of the syllabus in this style of karate. Tensing of the muscles and breath control can enable karateka to take blows to the body without coming to harm.*

2 *Heavy pots and other objects are employed to strengthen muscles in the hands and arms and other parts of the body.*

ginner must master these correctly to attain any worthwhile standard. In the original style there were no high kicks whatsoever, although today, with the advent of sport karate, some are now used. Traditionally, high kicks to the head were not employed because they were considered unsafe, with the line of balance too exaggerated.

Gogen Yamaguchi's thoughts on a lifetime spent in karate can be best summed up in his answer to the question: What is karate all about? He replied, 'Karate is not about fighting; it is about truth. The karate I teach cannot be understood without studying the Shinto religion and exploring yoga and then applying this knowledge to the art of karate itself.'

Uechi-ryu karate

Uechi-ryu karate can be said to be purely Okinawan, without any Japanese influence. It is thought that the roots of this system relate directly back to the Shaolin temple in China. The style's founder, Kanbun Uechi, studied in China at the Central temple in Fukien Province just before the turn of the century. It was here that he developed the principles of his own system, culling from the kung fu arts of the Tiger, Dragon and Crane. The Chinese name for this system was Pangai-noon, which means half hard, half soft.

This style of karate places strong emphasis on body conditioning so that a student can take all but the strongest kick or punch without losing balance or impairing his fighting spirit. Because of its kung fu background, it uses many circular movements.

Uechi-ryu karate has only eight kata in its repertoire, the most important of these being the Sanchin kata. Through rigorous practice of this kata, a student develops his body to withstand all manner of punches and kicks. Sanchin is known as the building block of the style. To test that students are performing this kata with the correct attitude and effort, and to see if they have acquired the right amount of muscular rigidity, they are kicked in the groin. Upon his death in 1948, Kanbun Uechi's son, Kanei, became head of the style.

Five against one
There is a story told about Kanbun Uechi, the founder of Uechi-ryu karate. It appears that while he was in China he visited a friend who lived as a recluse deep in the forest. As evening fell, Kanbun Uechi bade farewell to his friend and began the long walk home. Halfway home he was suddenly confronted by five tough-looking bandits, who threatened that if he had no money, then they would take his clothes. When Kanbun Uechi refused to disrobe, one of the bandits rushed at him. Calmly stepping aside, Kanbun deflected the blow and like lightning struck out himself. Instantly the bandit leader fell dead at his feet. The other four bandits looked on in amazement. Kanbun told the bandits to pick up their leader and dispose of him. He then asked if any of them wanted to try and take his clothes. Getting no response, Kanbun told the bandits that he had enjoyed the little confrontation, as he was becoming bored walking home alone. He said to the bandits that from now on he would be travelling this way home every night. So the next time they wanted to attack him, perhaps they would try and surprise him. That way, Kanbun went on, it would be more of a challenge to defend himself. He then turned and walked off.

Kanbun Uechi travelled that same path every night for a week, but he was never again troubled with bandits.

The karate training

The uniform that the student wears is called a karate-gi and is usually white in colour, though not always. The hall or club where the practitioners train is given the name of dojo. A dojo does not necessarily have to be indoors.

In the traditional arts certain etiquette procedures are upheld. For instance, prior to kumite (sparring) the student bows to his or her opponent as a mark of respect. At the beginning and end of a training session, after lining up, the whole class kneels and bows to the sensei (master).

All karate training consists of basic techniques, the foundation from which the various styles are built. From simple techniques the beginner is introduced to combinations, or the joining up of single movements into standardized patterns. To the western student the traditional emphasis on repetition of techniques in basic training does not always wear well. The reason for repeating a technique is to try and aim for perfection in its execution. Correct form and use of power leading to greater efficiency of movement are worked at during this constant repetition, and over a period of time these techniques become incorporated into the student's everyday movements, eventually becoming as natural as walking down the street.

Everyone coming into the martial arts

Above Sensei Enoeda, world-famous Shotokan karate instructor based in the UK, leads a class through one of the difficult Tekki katas.

starts at the bottom. Progress is made at an individual rate. Certain techniques may prove difficult to some, whereas others have little trouble in mastering them. It must always be remembered that karate is not a race. Because the basics take time to show obvious results, many modernists tend to look upon them as archaic and prefer to take short-cuts, thus defeating the object of the inner learning process. Serious character flaws are then encountered, which in turn lead to the eventual departure from the art.

The grading system

In the early days of Okinawan karate, grades were not deemed necessary, because in the eyes of the old masters you either succeeded or failed and there was no in-between. Even in Japan, there was only the white belt to denote the novice and the black belt to indicate a certain stage of proficiency.

The introduction of coloured belts has proved popular in the western world. Each provides a reward for achievement as well as a psychological incentive, while at the same time satisfying the ego. Normally most karate associations begin with a white belt, followed by a succession of different colours until the stage of shodan, or first dan black belt, is reached. The coloured belt stages are known as kyu grades. Examinations for levels of competency are usually conducted every three months, and the successful candidates then move on, for instance from eighth kyu to seventh, or from seventh kyu to sixth and so on. Each grading takes the student one step nearer the coveted black belt. Traditionally when coloured belts were first introduced wearers would start off with a light colour and then as they passed the next grading examination, they would dye the belt the relevant colour for the next level. Each time the colour would be a shade darker, until finally black was reached. An absolute beginner used to be given a red belt, then within a few weeks the student would take a simple preliminary test to achieve white belt standard.

The importance of kata

In simple terms a kata is a set pattern of movements in which the martial artist defends himself or herself against a series of

HEIAN GODAN

imaginary opponents. This exercise is aimed at developing timing, focus, balance and coordination. It is performed solo to enable the student to gain mastery over techniques without an instructor being present. Almost all schools of martial arts employ kata at some stage of teaching. Many of the Okinawan masters believed that the secret of karate lay within kata. In sporting tournaments and competitions the kata section is always hotly contested. Points are given for the best execution.

More importantly than just performing a series of sequences in the correct order is the understanding of the application of techniques. Many exponents spend their whole lives just perfecting the movements and mental awareness needed. Gichin Funakoshi believed that from kata every technique in karate can be learned.

This form is representative of the many katas that must be learnt for karate gradings, and takes about one minute to perform. It is from the Shotokan style.

la *Katas begins with yoi, the ready stance, with the feet slightly apart and the fists held in front of the thighs. The practitioner calls out the name of the kata.*

lb *The left foot is moved into back stance (kokutsu-dachi) and a left forearm block (chudan uchi-uke) is carried out against an imaginary opponent.*

2 *Without changing the stance a right reverse punch (gyaku-zuki) is executed, the movement being initiated from the hips.*

3 *The right foot is brought next to the left, the head is turned to the right and the left forearm is brought horizontally in front of the chest – all performed slowly.*

4 *Back stance is assumed by moving the right foot, and a right forearm block is executed.*

5 *A left reverse punch is carried out, without changing the back stance.*

6 The left foot is brought next to the right and the eyes to the front while the forearm is brought horizontally in front of the chest.

7 After swinging the fists from the left, a right forearm block is performed and the left fist is placed next to the right elbow. At the same time the right foot is moved forwards into back stance.

8 A step is made with the left foot into a low front stance (zenkutsu-dachi), while the fists are raised to the right and then thrust forward in a downward block with crossed wrists. This is to stop a low-level kick.

9 The hands are opened and thrust upwards quickly, wrists still crossed, to prevent a punch to the face. Meanwhile the front foot is pulled back slightly. The application of this move is shown in (1) opposite.

10a The wrists are rotated against each other and the hands are brought to the right side. The application of this move is shown in (2) opposite.

10b A strike is made with the left fist.

10c A strong punch is delivered with the right fist (chudan oi-zuki) while stepping forward with the right foot. Kiai!

11a The right foot is swung round 180° and the knee drawn upwards; the right fist is moved behind the ear. (The picture underneath shows this position from the rear.)

11b *The foot lands in horse-riding stance (kiba-dachi) while a right downward block is delivered (gedan-barai). (The picture to the right shows this position from the rear.)*

12a *While looking to the front the left hand is crossed under the right.*

1 *The opponent's punch to the face is blocked with a rising X-block, (jodan juji uke), as shown in step 9 of the kata.*

2 *The opponent is pulled forward off balance by the wrist—step 10a of the kata. This can be followed up with a punch from the left fist.*

12b **13a** **13b** **14** **15**

1 **2**

APPLICATION

1 The opponent's punch is blocked. See step 12b of the kata.

2 The opponent is pulled on to the crescent kick – step 13a of the kata.

3 Still pulling with the left hand, the opponent is now attacked with an elbow strike – step 13b of the kata.

3

16a

16b

17

18

19

 12b The left hand is slowly extended to perform an open-hand block. See application (1) far left.

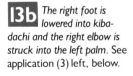 **13a** The right foot is swung forward in a crescent kick to hit the left palm. See application (2) left.

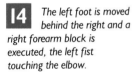 **13b** The right foot is lowered into kiba-dachi and the right elbow is struck into the left palm. See application (3) left, below.

14 The left foot is moved behind the right and a right forearm block is executed, the left fist touching the elbow.

15 The right arm is extended and the left foot is moved to the rear, toes just touching the ground (this view is taken from the side). See application (1) right.

16a A jump is performed, turning to the left and drawing the knees and feet high up. See application (2) below, right.

16b The landing is made with knees bent, performing a low X-block with crossed wrists. Kiai!

17 A long step is taken towards the rear into front stance (zenkutsu-dachi) together with a right forearm block, the left fist resting against the inside of the elbow.

18 The left foot is moved sideways to the right, the hands are opened and a low spear-hand strike (gedan nukite) is made to the front.

19 The weight is shifted into a back stance and a double block is made: a low gedan-barai with the left hand and a high jodan-uke with the right.

APPLICATION

1 Having blocked an attack from the right (step 15 of the kata) another opponent on the left raises a stick.

2 The upward leap shown in move 16a is to avoid the strike to the legs.

1

2

20 *Without moving the arms, the left foot is pulled in next to the right.*

21 *The body is twisted to face the opposite direction and the arms reversed.*

22 *A step is made with the right foot into front stance and a spear-hand attack is executed with the left hand. The right-hand palm faces the left ear.*

23 *The stance is changed into back stance and another double block is made: a low one with the right fist and a high one with the left.*

24 *The right foot is pulled back level with the left into a natural stance and the fists are held in front of the thighs. Yame (finish).*

Tamashiwara—the breaking power of karate

To the man in the street a karate expert conjures up in his mind's eye a person that can break a brick or slice through wood with his bare hands. This can be true, but power-breaking—or tamashiwara as it is known—is also a constructive tool for the improvement of one's karate.

In concentrating all his power upon one object, be it a concrete slab or a block of wood, the karateka is putting himself to the test, to measure his own ability and, in effect, his own self-confidence. He is overcoming the fear that his hands will be smashed to pieces as skin and bone crash through a solid object. It is necessary to overcome this fear factor to achieve success. The karateka is thus giving himself the opportunity to reflect upon the effects of his training, and how it has influenced his mind and body. Masatatsu Oyama once said, 'The karate that ignores breaking practice is no more useful than a fruit tree that bears no fruit.'

Some schools of karate toughen up their knuckles on a training device called a makiwara. This is usually a post embedded in the ground standing at a height of about four feet six inches (1.37m). The uppermost part is wrapped in layer after layer of straw. The karateka then pounds this post, day in and day out, to build up large callouses on his fist. Today, however, this is not actively encouraged in the West.

Various materials are used in tamashiwara challenges. Blocks of ice to concrete slabs have all been broken by karateka using their tamashiwara techniques. Masatatsu Oyama still holds the world record for breaking 33 roofing tiles with a single punch. Britain has had its fair share of power-breakers, where the most recent record was achieved with a power strike against 17 kerb stones made out of granite chips.

Kiai—the super shout of power

The kiai is a shout used when performing a technique in karate, usually at the moment of impact. The word means 'spirit meeting'. The sound must be initiated from the lower abdomen, with the exhalation of breath, and the cultivation of the skill requires proper control and timing. Executed correctly, it can stun an opponent momentarily, giving the attacker enough

Above It takes years of training and development of breaking techniques to smash this many slabs. The elbow can be used as well as the fist, palm-heel or knife-hand.

Left A well-focused 'kiai' can literally stun an opponent. All karateka learn this technique right from the start of their training.

time to make a decisive strike. This blood-curdling sound, together with the accompanying contraction of muscles, brings a surge of energy to the user, providing extra impulse. Weightlifters often emit such noises just at the moment of the lift.

In the East, it is believed that the abdomen is the source of all power.

The advent of sport karate

Probably the single biggest promoter of karate has been the advent of sporting tournaments. This has the twofold purpose of allowing karate practitioners to pit their abilities against those of their peers under competition rules, while also permitting audiences to witness the spectacle. Sporting competition creates stars, and stars encourage fans. Within a short time there was a vibrant tournament scene.

Karate competition developed in Japan, but in the early 70s it was the Europeans and the Americans who encouraged it. An organization was established to govern karate on a world scale, known as the World Union of Karate-do Organizations,

or WUKO. Over 48 member countries take part in bi-annual world championships. Great Britain has the distinction of being the only country in the world to win the world championship on three separate occasions. The coach manager for the British team was London-based David 'Ticky' Donovan, who has been classed by Europeans and Japanese alike as the greatest coach in the world.

It seems inevitable that as the sporting aspects were stressed in karate, groups would splinter away and form separate off-shoots. Karate seems to have been bugged by this problem during modern times. In the USA they took karateka, put boxing gloves on their hands and padded boots on their feet, and a new sport was born—that of full contact karate. In this sport contestants actually land full-force strikes on their opponents in a boxing ring. This particular sport appeared to take off virtually overnight. An organization was quickly established to oversee the running of events, called the PKA or Professional Karate Association. As it turned out, full contact karate overtook the amateur scene in America in a big way.

A lighter form of this sport, without the full contact kicks and punches, is called semi-contact. This particular sport is becoming increasingly popular worldwide.

Women in the martial arts

Women are so often termed the gentle sex in this chauvinistic male-orientated world of ours. The fighting arts would seem far removed from the lives of most women, and yet surprisingly ladies have taken to the practice of martial arts in a big way and achieved amazing results. At first women were not allowed to take part in active competition (free fighting), but constant petitioning eventually gained them a slot. Prior to this, they were only permitted to enter tournaments in the kata sections. Success in competition has led to women opening their own karate clubs and teaching men. Although not too widespread at the moment, women are now getting the recognition they deserve on the current karate scene.

Most women begin training in the martial arts for the purpose of self-defence, although some do enrol simply as a way of keeping fit. Certain factors do have to be overcome if a woman is to succeed. Inbred conditioning that women 'don't fight' or that fighting is un-ladylike, are obstacles that have to be surmounted. In these days

Below Three world champions of karate with their coach 'Ticky' Donovan. At the end of four days of competition in Maastricht, Holland, 1984, Great Britain had won the team kumite (sparring) event for an unprecedented third time. They had also taken three individual gold medals, one silver and two bronze. Much of the credit for this astonishing performance can be given to their coach.

of change and equal opportunities women are making more inroads into the martial arts, and are winning medals in the world championships.

Fear or anger can often be a woman's motivating force in looking to the martial arts for self-defence training. No longer are they willing to become victims, easy targets for mindless rapists. Now they can have the skills to fight back. For many women the martial arts can provide that essential training. As is often said, 'Fear of men turns women into victims.'

It is strange that men still view women as a kind of protected species, and yet women have played a vital role in the history of martial arts, as is evidenced by Yim Wing Chun's invention of the art that bears her name.

Western attitudes

It can be seen that the eastern methods of fighting are still undergoing a constant evolution. Western scientific research into athletic endeavours is in some cases taking karate away from its early traditions, placing much more emphasis on peak performance based on the principles of special nutrition, coaching and systemized circuit-training, in the hope that the very best can be extracted from athletes. This does raise the question: Are we in the West losing sight of the true aims of karate-do?

69

THE WEAPON ARTS OF JAPAN

'To know the outcome, look to the root. Study the past to know the future.'

Many of today's martial arts were once battlefield skills, devised for the sole purpose of inflicting injury and death against an adversary. Because warfare has changed considerably in the last hundred years, these once ancient skills have been transformed into artistic disciplines.

In the Japanese arsenal of fighting arts, a certain amount of confusion arises between 'jutsu' and 'do', as in kenjutsu and kendo. A 'do' when used as a suffix to a martial discipline, such as in karate-do or aikido, means a road, a way, a path. Traditionally, when used in this context, it means the pathway to self-understanding and perfection through the training system of a particular martial art. Some of the old martial ways have been developed or adapted to place special emphasis upon such personal enlightenment. If 'jutsu' is the suffix, this indicates an art or skill, but refers to the warrior ways of the samurai class and the expression of their intentions in combat. The main difference between the old styles and the new is that victory in combat was to the samurai an absolute priority.

Today's young people who practise martial arts tread the path (do) and learn that, although fighting releases violent energy, under disciplined conditions they can channel that same force inwardly, and let the teachings of martial arts become a vehicle for personal development, tempering the spirit and uniting mind and body, so that they may, in turn, benefit modern society with their new-found maturity.

Kendo—the way of the sword

Kendo, meaning way of the sword, is a martial art developed from the classical Japanese kenjutsu. Kenjutsu had no sporting considerations; its sole aim was to kill an enemy. Kendo history is the history of the samurai, the warrior class of feudal Japan, whose basic weapon was the katana or long sword. The sword in Japan was held with such high regard, that it was sometimes known as the 'soul of the warrior'. No one can seriously study kendo without coming into contact with that

70

Left *Two actors portray the samurai Kameo Maru and Ario Maru caught up in the events of the wars of the 12th century. In this duel the figure on the right uses a thrusting action which is parried by the man on the left who reinforces his defence with a hand on the back of his sword.*

Below *A general from the Tokugawa family (on the right) defends his encampment against a vicious onslaught. His emblem is repeated on his jinbaori (war coat) which he wears. Like the others in full armour, he wears a tachi – a sword slung with the edge down. The attacking retainers are wielding yari (long spears) which were typical of mass armies.*

which lies beneath the surface, beyond technique.

Originally fencing was taught with a live (real) blade and then around AD 400 a training device was introduced called a bokuto. This was a piece of heavy red oak with the shape, weight and balance of a real sword and soon this became a popular weapon to practise with. Fencing in those days was taught by means of kata, devised by the school's master, to simulate actual fighting situations. Although quite revolutionary for the times, training with the bokuto still caused injury. The next stage of

71

development was the introduction of the shinai, along with protective armour. A shinai is made of four bamboo strips held together at strategic points by cord and at the ends by leather, one forming the handle. A handguard protects the fingers. With this equipment blows could actually be struck on the opponent. This allowed the student the facility to try complex multiple techniques time and time again, without the risk of the shinai smashing into his opponent's head or body if he failed.

Miyamoto Musashi was born in 1584, the son of a fencing master. At the age of 13 he killed his first man, a rival fencing master who had had an argument with Musashi's father and insulted him. As Musashi grew older it was obvious that he had a great talent with swords. He was placed under the tutelage of several kendo masters, until Musashi's skill knew no bounds. It is said that in his lifetime he fought 60 duels and never lost one, with the possible exception of the legend related below. Musashi cared little for fame and fortune; he seemed intent upon spending his life searching for perfection. Many famous swordsmen of the day sought him out to test his ability with a blade.

Miyamoto Musashi originated new concepts in fencing, and devised a special technique for the long and short sword known as the two-sword style or Niten-ichi-ryu. Labelled Japan's greatest swordsman, Musashi was also very artistically gifted in calligraphy and painting. He wrote a book that is still read today, called *Go Rin No Sho* or the *Book of Five Rings*, translated into English for the first time in 1974 by Victor Harris. This book is a

Below *In Japan there has been a tremendous revival of interest in the ancient art of kendo. Here two kendoka are practising in a Japanese dojo. The Japanese characters to be seen on the kendoka's tare give his name and above them (concealed by his gloves) is given the place he is from. This identification label is known as a zekken.*

valuable treatise on mental discipline and is used by today's businessmen in Japan as a guide to strategy.

Musashi was convinced he was invincible and spent his life proving he was. An old legend relates that Musashi was only ever beaten once in his lifetime, and in that particular duel he fought with bokuto instead of live blades. His adversary was a man named Muso Gonnosuke, also a great swordsman, and the originator of the 4ft 2in (1.25m) stick known as the jo. Gonnosuke had engaged Musashi in a friendly match and was soundly beaten. Somewhat depressed at this Gonnosuke retired to a Shinto shrine and meditated. It was here that the idea for the long stick is said to have come to him. Gonnosuke experimented with the jo for months, applying all his fencing knowledge and other martial weapons experience, until he finally devised a series of techniques which he named Shindo Muso Ryu 'jutsu. At their next meeting, a second challenge was issued to Musashi, which he accepted. But even with his two-sword techniques Musashi could not beat the old man with the 4ft 2in (1.25m) stick and consequently lost the only fight in his long career. Gonnosuke, from that day on concentrated solely on perfecting the jo to improve its techniques.

Miyamoto Musashi died a natural death in 1645 at the age of 61.

At the beginning of the Meiji restoration, in 1868, an edict was issued banning the wearing of all swords in public. This edict was instrumental in making kendo more acceptable as a method of self-discipline, and the art rose to new heights of popularity. Later on the Japanese Ministry of Education passed a regulation that made kendo (or judo) compulsory in public and private schools in Japan. Kendo's character-building qualities provided the purpose for introducing it into the classroom.

Modern kendo emerges

In the aftermath of World War II General MacArthur of the US occupying forces banned kendo. But in 1951 the ban was lifted and kendo was re-introduced into secondary schools. Kendo in pre-war Japan had been actively encouraged by the government; now the interest of Japan's post-war youth had to be awakened. Slowly kendo gained ground and eventually became as popular as ever. Active competition was encouraged at home and internationally, and the spread of worldwide interest led to a governing body being set up in Japan. Rules of competition were established, together with a series of katas.

Kendo today is very much different from the form practised a hundred years ago in Japan. Certain schools of thought decry this, saying that it has been diluted and become ineffective. Nevertheless, kendo's popularity is on the increase.

Equipment

The costume of the kendoka consists of a cotton jacket, and an ankle-length split skirt known as a hakama. The armour, or bogu, consists of a tare which is a waist-and-groin protector, and the do (breastplate) made of either fibre or bamboo covered in leather and lacquered. A wide headband, called tenugui, is wrapped around the head to soak up the perspiration and prevent it from running into the eyes. Next comes the face mask, or men; this is rigidly constructed from steel or nickel with grille-like bars running horizontally across the face. The final piece of equipment is the kote, a kind of glove resembling a gauntlet, to protect the hands from blows. A certain amount of ritual is observed when donning the uniform.

In kendo competition there are eight

Below *There is a standard procedure for putting on the armour for kendo practice. It is always performed in a kneeling position.*

KENDO ARMOUR

1 *First to be put on is the tare, or apron. Tightly stitched layers of felt and fabric protect the vital points below the waist from accidental blows.*

2 *The do (breast plate) is tied over this, across the shoulders and around the waist. It is formed from bamboo or fibre and covered with leather and lacquered.*

3 *The tenugui is wrapped and folded over the head as shown and makes the wearing of the helmet considerably more comfortable.*

4 *Long flat cords secure the men (helmet) on the head. At the front a reinforced pad protects the throat from thrusts.*

techniques that can score points: seven of them are blows and one a thrust. The blows are indicative of blade-cutting motions, although in competition a shinai is of course used. The kendo thrust must be strongly directed to the throat. Whereas in karate competition the rules are hard to define to the uninitiated, and the scoring even harder, in kendo it is quite straightforward: when a blow is struck at a specific area, the name of the place struck is shouted out, thus enabling the spectator to follow the match. Kendo competition does not allow blows or cuts to the legs.

Great emphasis in kendo is placed upon the footwork, which is regarded as second only to the eyesight. After the student learns the basic kendo sword strokes and stances, he or she advances on to surburi, consisting of cutting exercises practised by oneself (similar to shadow boxing).

In kendo the first real grade is the shodan (first degree black belt), although some instructors give kyu grades to their students as an incentive to progress. Despite this, there is no outward identification of grading at all. The only way to distinguish standards is through fencing. Progress is made at the individual's own pace of accomplishment. To advance from beginner to black belt first dan can take anything up to five years or as little as one.

Once a beginner has acquired the knowledge of basic techniques, he or she adv-

ances to the next stage which is practising with an opponent. This is done either with another student or directly with the instructor. To enable the beginner actually to get the feel of really hitting an object, training is sometimes carried out on a device known as a knocking stick or post. This reinforces basic training learnt right from the start, such as tightening of the grip and also, upon impact, keeping a well-balanced posture. The knocking post can perhaps be likened to karate's makiwara.

Once mastery of the basics has been achieved, the kendoka tends to favour certain techniques over others, depending on personal physique preferences.

On occasion, kendoka will compete with two 'swords'. One of them is the standard shinai and the other is smaller, approximately 22 inches (55cm). This form of combat requires much skill. The name given to this type of fighting is called Nito, whose meaning is two swords, derived from Musashi's school of fencing.

All the major religions of Japan, especially Zen Buddhism, left their influence on the art. Kendo became a way of attaining inner peace. A kendo master can walk away from a fight still keeping his dignity and self-respect intact. There are many different schools of kendo, but in the final analysis all offer a path to self-development, though they may differ slightly on how to get there.

KENDO POINTS

In kendo, seven blows can win points: three to the head (men points), two to the wrists (kote points) and two to the chest (do). However, no points are awarded unless the competitor shows ki-ken-tai (spirit, sword and body).

1 The right wrist, being the nearest, is open to attack at all times.

2 A cut to the side of the head wins a men point.

3 The only thrust that can score is this one, to the throat.

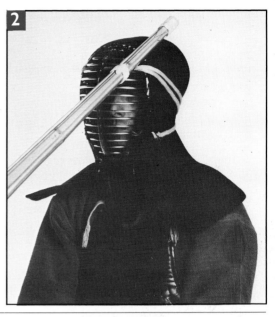

Left *The grip constitutes an important part of kendo basics. The kendoka on the left is aiming to score a men point (cut to the head) on his opponent.*

Iai-do—the art of drawing the sword

Iai-do is a twentieth-century development of the art of iai-jutsu or batto-jutsu. The invention of the art of batto-jutsu as a distinctive part of the wider study of swordsmanship, kenjutsu, is generally attributed to Hayashizaki Jinsuke Shigenobu. Shigenobu lived about 400 years ago in the province of Oshu.

Batto can be translated as 'striking from the sheath' and the art of batto, or iai-jutsu as it became known, soon gained popularity as a specialization of a number of kenjutsu schools (ryu).

The years of peace that ensued during the Edo period have to a certain extent diluted the original combat effectiveness of iai and emphasized the character-building aspect of the art. The emergence of iai as a 'do' form in this century is seen by many as an evolutionary development of the older styles.

In the ancient iai-jutsu, the objective was both offensive and defensive. It taught the warrior to go into action instantly upon a sudden encounter. Striking on the draw distinguishes iai-jutsu within kenjutsu; the earlier schools of sword-fighting placed no great importance on the drawing of the blade but rather on its effectiveness when unsheathed.

With the unification of Japan under the Emperor Meiji, the feudal period of Japan was over. The edict from the throne that saw the abolition of the wearing of swords by the samurai, also saw the abandonment of many of the martial skills that had been bred into this warrior class for countless generations. The art of kenjutsu fell into decline as the samurai turned to other areas of occupation for Japan had entered the modern era and was hungry for industrialization to catch up with the rest of the world. However, although swords had been banned, the warrior did not need an opponent to practise iai-jutsu; this could be done alone. Slowly the combative aspects of the many schools of iai-jutsu became absorbed and students concerned themselves with training as a means of personal development of mind, body and spirit. Thus, iai-jutsu eventually became iai-do.

Modern iai-do

Although iai-do practice should be aesthetically pleasing, all the techniques are firmly based on a practical foundation. A full iai technique combines the draw and cut with the quick return into the scabbard. The

sword is worn in the belt with the cutting edge facing upwards to enable the draw and cut to become virtually a single action.

After paying his respects to the shrine within the dojo, the swordsman sits back on his haunches in a typically Japanese position. His next gesture is to bow to his sword which is positioned in front of him. This respect truly exemplifies the high regard the Japanese hold for the katana.

Today in Japan there are many schools of iai, but every school adheres to the basic principles which can be divided into four parts. First is nukitsuke, which is the actual drawing of the blade from its scabbard. Then comes Kritsuke, the cut, followed by chiburi, or the symbolic shaking of the blood from the blade after a successful cut. Finally there is noto, the returning of the blade to its scabbard. The principle behind noto is to return the blade quickly without casting the eyes downwards, while remaining alert. This latter part requires perfect precision since the slightest mistake can result in damage to the hands on the razor-sharp blade. Novices may train with dull-edged swords for years before progressing on to a live blade.

From time to time competitions are held in which two contestants perform in parallel and comparative levels of skill are judged.

Above right Ishido Sensei, one of the foremost exponents of ia-ido, in the classic posture of jodan no kamae. The photograph was taken at the All Japan Iai Competition.

78

The naginata—women's weapon of defence

The naginata resembles a pole with a short curved knive on the end, very similar to a halberd. It is about 6ft 6in (2m) in length and is made of wood. Its curved blade measures about 20 inches (50cm) and is extremely sharp. Use of the naginata as a weapon on the battlefields of Japan dates back more than a thousand years. A man armed with one had a terrific advantage over a swordsman. Not only could it outreach a sword, but it also had a tremendous sweeping capability. When an opponent evaded the razor-sharp blade, the user could whip the butt end around and sweep the opponent off his feet and then decapitate him. The bushi (Japanese feudal warriors) also found that the naginata had a distinct advantage over the spear (yari), because when used with a circular motion it could inflict deadly slashes on all parts of an enemy's anatomy. It became so effective that a shin protector was introduced as a standard part of the armour, as many a warrior in the past had lost his legs due to the slicing power of this formidable weapon.

With the modernization of battle weapons the naginata, like the bow, fell into disuse. Interestingly enough, it was the wives of the warriors who next adopted the weapon. It was modified and used as a training weapon for teaching discipline to the girls of the bushi families. As the females mastered this shortened version of the weapon it was found to be of great use around the home, especially when their husbands rode off to participate in some war. Skill in the use of the naginata proved

Left Unlike kendo, naginata-do allows cuts to the legs. Traditionally used by women for self-defence, the naginata can be a formidable weapon in expert hands. The naginata in this picture is made of wood and is used for the performance of kata.

Above In 1985 Grandmaster Soke Tsuyoshi Munetoshi Inouye delighted his English audience with a performance of sword drawing using his 400-year-old katana.

an excellent defence for the women when attacked or molested by the many roving bands of robbers and ronins (masterless samurai) during this turbulent era. Japanese homes of the period had low ceilings, so this shortened naginata could be used indoors as well as outside.

At the emergence of Japan as a modern nation, the naginata was kept alive as an art form. Naginata training was deemed an essential part of the proper upbringing for a young lady. During the period leading up to World War II, the naginata was eagerly encouraged by the government as a form of important military training for women. After the great conflict the naginata began its rebirth with the modification of some of the martial concepts, and sporting aspects were introduced. The naginata became a do. The live blade was replaced with an angled piece of plaited bamboo and naginata-do was soon a popular female sport. The kata in naginata-do are circular, not linear. The sport is said to be beneficial for a woman's body because it develops the muscles evenly, providing the body with flexiblity and suppleness, thus encouraging good all-round tone.

There are two schools of naginata-do, the Tendo or heavenly way, and the Shinkage or new shadow school. The standard uniform for the women is the same as in kendo: the keikogi (the literal meaning of this is practice wear) and hakama—a kind of split skirt. In competition male kendoka have pitted their sword skills against the ladies of the naginata, and nearly always come off second best. The female exponent cannot hope to match the strength of a male kendoka, so instead she places emphasis on speed and flexibility. This, combined with a high degree of skill through years of training, puts the men on the run, time and time again. Women's colleges throughout Japan all have regular classes for training in naginata-do.

Kyudo—the zen archery of Japan

Of all the Japanese weapon arts none is perhaps more steeped in Zen Buddhism than that of kyudo, the way of the bow. As in the other arts, kyudo came from a battlefield skill, that of kyujutsu, but with the introduction of firearms in the sixteenth century the bow, or yumi, became obsolete as part of the arsenal of the samurai.

In kyudo the archer pits himself against only one opponent—himself. The goals in Zen archery are typical of all Zen teachings. They are as elusive as trying to catch the wind in your hands, because in the end the archer can truly have no goals. The bow, arrow, target and archer must fuse together to become one. Then, and only then, will the kyudoka (one who practises kyudo) release the arrow. Even at this stage, with the arrow in flight, hitting the target is not important. The vital considerations are how the shooting is done, and the archer's state of mind when the arrow is released. Style and the method of preparation are important factors in kyudo. It is only of secondary concern that the arrow actually hits the target. As the old saying in kyudo states, 'To achieve the proper style in kyudo is to glimpse the mastery of life itself.'

The art is performed with a ritualized exactness, and yet only a few are able to achieve the ultimate knowledge of enlightenment that makes them masters of the art. In a meditative pose the archer concentrates upon the proper state of mind. The slightest variation in the execution of style, or an improper attitude, can only bring failure. The beauty of this form of martial arts lies in its ability to expand the precepts of the fighting arts beyond that of actually bearing down on an opponent physically.

Without actually being involved in kyudo, it is difficult for the onlooker to understand the values of the archer and his aims. At times it even appears a little contradictory, for without a relaxed attitude and correct motions, without personal concern for hitting the target, the arrow will simply not find its mark. The archer will have failed. On the other hand if he observes all the correct rituals and procedures and by chance accidentally hits the bull's eye, but deep down in his heart of hearts knows that the movements were performed without the proper spirit of concentration, then once again, he will have failed. It is not true Zen. He cannot even pretend that everything was in order, because in doing so he is only fooling himself, which once again is not true Zen.

The bow and arrow
The bow in kyudo is the longest in the world, measuring over six feet (1.8m). The grip is not centred, but is approximately one-third of the distance from the bottom of the bow. No other shaped bow can be found in either Europe or Asia that even remotely resembles the Japanese yumi. Traditionally the bow was constructed entirely out of bamboo, with a pull weight of around 80 pounds (36kg). It is a com-

Right *After the passing of the great age of the samurai, their feats and exploits were often depicted by actors, especially in the 18th and 19th centuries. Here Homomura Hyakutaro performs the role of the samurai Wada Raihachi.*

和田雷八

百尋吉三師

pound bow, which means it is made up of strips of wood laminated, unlike the old English long bow which is classed as a single stick and made from yew. With the grip of the kyudo bow closer to the bottom than that of its European counterparts, there is the added advantage of increased strength.

There are two main schools of kyudo which are Ogasawara and Heki. The Ogasawara school developed along ceremonial lines and was noted for its high draw and emphasis on formal kata. This style is the most universally practised in Japan today. A splinter group was set up in the sixteenth century which led to the formation of the Heki-ryu, who concentrated upon kyudo for more practical purposes.

The eight stages

All styles divide the act of shooting into hassetsu or eight stages. The first movement is ashibumi meaning to step or tread. This is part of the archer's stance, with the feet separated and the body turned at a right-angle to the target. The kyudoka carries no quiver, unlike his western counterpart. Usually only one or two arrows are used. One is held ready for shooting and the second is held in the string hand and secured by the little finger. The next stage is dozukuri, the positioning of the upper body, with the torso held straight but relaxed and breathing controlled. Then comes yugamae, which is setting the bow in place with the arrow in a firing position. This is followed by uchiokoshi, a double-sectioned stage in which the kyudoka lifts the bow and looks at the target for the first time, then looks away; these movements are respectively termed monomi and daisan. Next begins the draw, called hiki-wake, with the string hand pulling the arrow all the way back behind the ear. This position is held while the archer meditates on all the correct procedures; this is termed the kiai meaning the meeting. Now the archer waits for the arrow to shoot itself: the moment arrives when the strain is too great on the archer's thumb holding the string. The hanare, or release, is then fulfilled. The archer does not willingly release the arrow; it just happens. With the arrow in flight the archer watches it winging its way to the target, or not to the target. This motionless stance is known as zanshin, the moment of knowledge. If the acquired skills are possessed by the kyudoka, then it is at this stage that enlightenment takes place.

All these eight stages must be adhered to with complete attention to precision, performed in a totally relaxed state. Students who embrace the art of kyudo as their own way to Zen enlightenment, must be prepared for years of training. As progress in kyudo is considerably slower than in the more energetic martial arts, archers usually reach their peak of ability in their seventies and even eighties.

Kyudo in modern Japan is growing at a rapid rate, especially the battlefield style of Haiki Ryu, recognized by a low bow hold. It is interesting to note that the bow and arrow in Japanese folk legend symbolize the flight of time. Because of this arrowheads are sold to the people as talismans at Shinto shrines on New Year's morning.

Yabusame

During wars of feudal times, archers rode on horseback while releasing arrows in a rapid progression from all sides. This skill is called yabusame. Horseback archery was strongly influenced by the Shinto religion.

Above A young Japanese kyudoka concentrates on the moment when the arrow will release itself and become one with its target.

Today, annual yabusame contests are still held in the grounds of Shinto shrines, such as the Hachiman shrine at Kamakura and the Meiji shrine in Tokyo. In yabusame, the archers gallop along a 280-yard (256m) course, and shoot at five evenly spaced targets set up on poles. In days gone by, the Hachiman shrine used to attract samurai from all over Japan to compete against each other, like knights in a jousting tournament in medieval Europe. Modern sporting tournaments of yabusame involve all the competitors dressing in the ancient samurai costumes before taking part.

Okinawan weapons

The sai

The sai is a weapon that resembles a trident, but with characteristics of a thick dagger. Traditionally Okinawa was thought to be its home, but weapons of marked similarity exist all over the East. It is a three-pronged truncheon about 15 to 20 inches (38 to 50cm) in length. Mostly used as a defensive instrument against various weapons such as the sword and the long staff, its great popularity in recent years has been due largely to karate practitioners who, after achieving their black belt dan grade, use the sai and other weapons as an extension of their training. The sai are used in pairs; sometimes a third is placed behind the back, wedged into the karate belt. This spare was originally intended for throwing at the enemy in a time of crisis, leaving the other two for defensive work. The weapon is used to block, strike, thrust or ensnare. In training with the sai there is no competition and it is practised according to classical traditions in order to keep its intrinsic values. As the sai are made of metal, deflection techniques can be used against a sword with a live blade, in addition to a trapping movement which involves wedging the sword blade in between the tines of the sai.

A sai can be held in one of two ways, either by the hilt or tsuka, or with the prongs resting down the inside of the forearm. The adept, when attacked, can flick his wrist and the long pointed shaft of the sai appears as if from nowhere.

The nunchaku or rice flails

The nunchaku is a weapon consisting of two lengths of wood joined by either chain or cord which makes a universal joint and it can be used like a whip or flail. It came into prominence with the advent of the Chinese martial arts movies in the early seventies, and of course the late Bruce Lee. The authorities, quick to notice their abuse in the hands of hooligans, brought in legislation and it was classed as an offensive weapon.

Nunchakus have been part of the martial arts scene for a few hundred years. Originally they were used for flailing rice from the husks, but later adopted as a weapon. Nunchaku is practised in kata form and has defensive and offensive techniques. Accuracy and control are the most important aspects of training and much time is spent perfecting these. In training, only the type with the cord is used, as the chain variety is deemed best used against other weapons, for defence.

Until quite recently the nunchaku was

Left *Generally used in pairs, the sai can be held with the main prong lying along the forearm, giving good control for defensive work against other weapons.*

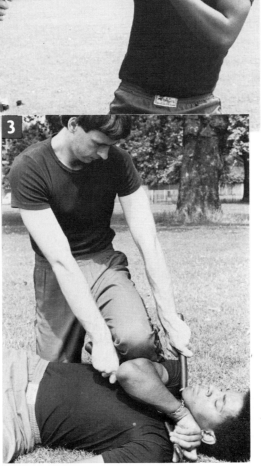

only ever practised for the improvement of the karateka, at a personal and individual level, but now a sporting element has been introduced whereby two exponents wearing special padded armour for protection actually go out on to the contest floor and do battle with each other. This is known as *nunchaku de combat* and originated in France. Its popularity has been far reaching, and now many countries in Europe are staging regular competitions. The equipment consists of padded gauntlet gloves, a face mask not unlike that worn by kendoka, a padded breast plate and specially designed nunchaku that bend upon impact. These are constructed from a foam rubber material and are quite safe. Points in the contest are given for disarmings (taking the nunchaku off your opponent by means of a strike—sweeps and take-downs are also included). By its very nature, nunchaku competition is conducted at an almost lightning pace.

The power of the nunchaku comes from its use of centrifugal force to whip out one of the shafts and the impact power is quite tremendous. In addition to the flailing techniques, this weapon can also be used to strangle, and cripple joints.

The tonfa and kama

The tonfa or tui-fa was another Okinawan farming implement that was adapted by the peasants as a weapon, to be used against their Japanese invaders. Originally it was a handle with the purpose of turning the wheel of a manually operated millstone that ground rice. Most commonly the tonfa is used like the sai as one of a pair, with one in each hand. The weapon consists of a long hardwood shaft with a cylindrical grip placed six inches (15cm) from the end at a right-angle. With the weapon held by this projection each shaft lies along the underside of the forearm and is used to block and parry attacks. The grip can be revolved to allow the shafts to spin outwards to strike an enemy in the temple or throat.

The kama is quite simply an agricultural sickle and has been in use as long as man has grown crops. By itself it is obviously a formidable weapon, but in the hands of an expert it is quite lethal. The blade is attached to a long handle which is flared slightly at the butt to prevent the hands from slipping on to the razor-sharp crescent-shaped blade. As with most of these Okinawan weapons, the kama can be used either singly or in pairs. The user can chop, hook and strike with various combinations, to put an adversary in deadly trouble.

NUNCHAKU

 As the attacker strikes out with a knife, the defender quickly jumps to the side, at the same time striking downwards to the attacker's wrist with double nunchaku.

 The defender ensnares the attacker's knife arm with the nunchaku chain and twists upwards. The attacker's knife blade is forced in on himself and he eventually loses his balance and falls.

3 The defender can now counter.

84

The stick arts of Japan

In twelfth-century England the quarter staff was as common as the bow and arrow, yet today there are no fighting systems based on it still in existence, whereas in the East we find a comprehensive selection of techniques involving sticks or staffs of varying lengths. In Japan there are basically three types of fighting stick. The bo staff is around six feet (1.8m) in length and has an incredible 350 fighting styles in its repertoire. Next is the jo which is a little over 4ft 2in (1.25m) long and has 70 fighting systems attached to it. Finally there is the hanbo, which is three feet (90cm) long. Han means half, so it is half the size of the bo.

The simple stick does not conjure up all the glamour of the other weapons in the martial arts' arsenal, and yet, armed with a simple stick, Muso Gonnosuke defeated the greatest swordsman in Japan—which must surely prove that it is the man behind the weapon and not the weapon itself that is the critical factor.

One of the popular stick schools in Japan is that of Shindo Muso Ryu. Their core weapon is the four-foot jo stick. The wood is of Japanese oak and is not kiln-dried, but dried naturally, as kiln-drying takes out too much of the natural water content, leaving the wood light and easily broken. The stick is about an inch (2.5cm) thick and very, very strong. In fact jodo is practised against a wooden training sword, as used against a live blade the jo would either shatter or bend it. The jodo techniques consist of thrusts, strikes, blocks and blows. In some techniques the sword can be taken clean from the opponent's hand by just hitting the blade at the correct angle.

The first thing the student learns is called kihon or basic techniques. In jodo there is no contest, only perfection of technique and ability to master the sticks. You train to temper your fighting spirit.

The bo staff is familiar as a weapon in virtually every fighting system in the world. It needs no modification for combat and was used as a long-range weapon. Terrifying force can be generated by this long pole-like weapon in the hands of an expert.

Within the spectrum of Japanese martial arts weapons, there are many other strange and wonderful implements that have been used in one way or another as tools for fighting. The jitte, or iron truncheon, was once popular and used by the police force. It resembled the sai, but only had one tine at the hilt. The iron war fan, known as the tessen, was another flamboyant battlefield weapon. Ingenuity knew no bounds, where methods of killing and fighting were concerned. Each weapon was studied and dissected for possible flaws before it was put to use in a training regimen. When that particular weapon was mastered, another one was introduced.

Right *A dramatic moment from a kata employing the bo staff.*

JAPANESE UNARMED DEFENCE SYSTEMS

'Excellence does not remain alone; it is sure to attract neighbours.'

Western students of martial arts cannot fail to appreciate that no matter what style or type they train in, somewhere along that long road they will see things that to normal men would seem impossible to envisage. That winding path is paved with individuals who appear to defy the laws of physics, medicine, even gravity itself. To try and explain, or even work out some logical reasoning behind the amazing feats performed by masters of the martial arts, would surely prove an impossibility. To put into words a martial heritage and philosophical thought that stretches back more than a thousand years cannot be done. But perhaps through practising those arts ourselves, immersing ourselves in such an endeavour, we can at least gain an insight by walking that same path, like so many have done before, remembering Confucius's famous words that 'the journey of a thousand miles begins with the first step'.

Aikido

Aikido was founded by Morihei Uyeshiba in 1942. Aikido means the way of harmony. In this art there is no actual attack as such, the basic ethic being defence first. The attacker should be overcome by the aikido-ka or aiki-ist (one who practises aikido) using the minimum of force without inflicting any serious injuries. All feelings of aggression must be pushed aside. The throws in aikido are executed by utilizing wrist and armlocks. Distancing is also very essential. All practitioners are required to maintain a pacifist attitude.

Morihei Uyeshiba was the eldest son of a farmer, and being a sickly child he was encouraged to learn martial arts to build up his strength. So Uyeshiba began the study of jiu-jitsu; when he was 19 he was struck down with scarlet fever, which left him severely weakened. In an effort to build back his strength he enrolled in Yagyu Shinkage Ryu Jujutsu. During the Russo-Japanese war Uyeshiba was conscripted into the army. This gave him ample opportunity to travel and study other forms of martial arts and combat methods.

After the war, returning to jujutsu, Uyeshiba was made a master instructor with the title Menkyo-kaiden, which is the highest licence of proficiency. After that achievement he began to travel all around Japan trying out other systems. In 1915 he began studies in yet another style of jujutsu, that of Daito-ryu, under the great master Sokaku. Here, too, after many years of diligent endeavour he was awarded his master's certificate in that system. But Uyeshiba was dissatisfied with the strictly militaristic styles he had been learning, and left to seek higher ideals. He had a deep abiding love for traditional martial arts and his constant studies into martial systems were the driving force towards realization of his ultimate goal: that was to revive the spiritual quality of budo (fighting ways) by training and still more training.

The death of his father in 1920 came as a great shock and left Uyeshiba in a state of psychological distress. He sought the spiritual guidance of a priest named Deguchi of the Omoto sect (a branch of Shintoism). Under the priest's guidance he meditated and studied philosophy. It was during this period of being close to nature that he is said to have had a vision of enlightenment. Apparently Uyeshiba had just finished a period of intense meditation. Walking out into a small yard he knelt to take a drink. Suddenly the ground began to tremble, causing ripples in the soil. Right in front of him a stream of vapour shot out of the ground like a geyser. He was bathed in a golden liquid which covered his whole body. His body felt light as though he were

87

floating and the laws of gravity seemed not to exist. Voices were ringing in his ears, but as he looked around he could only see the birds chirping. At that moment Morihei Uyeshiba knew that he and the universe were entwined. The message he received was that the fundamental principle of the martial arts was love and not combat, love of the universal kind. The martial arts of the true way were not about brute force and injury, but harmony and the promotion of the ki (intrinsic energy likened to the chi). This revelation changed Uyeshiba's thinking dramatically, and was to be the foundation that aikido was built upon.

Returning to Tokyo, Uyeshiba opened his first dojo in 1927. In February 1942 aikido was officially recognized as the name of his new art. Thus, with his way of harmony, Uyeshiba accomplished his burning desire to keep alive the legacy of budo in the modern world.

The principles

Just as with Zen, one only understands aikido by practising it. The art appears to encompass the trinity of Buddhism, Shintoism and Confucianism, but as always, Eastern philosophy throws up contradictions. Many individuals consider Buddhism and Confucianism to be opposing philosophies, but let us not forget that it was the Buddhist priests who introduced Confucian doctrines to Japan. For the major part we must look to the Shinto religion as aikido's root philosophy, for without understanding this, aikido's means of harnessing the force of the universe will not be comprehensible. Shintoism expresses the love of nature, of life's processes, the delight in nature's rhythms. Uyeshiba believed that aikido was a natural expression of our existence, a free expression of our life force and a way towards harmony with nature. Thus, through aikido, mind and body are united with spiritual harmony and universal love.

In the technique of the art, being passive is the correct defence. A beginner is taught to blend with his or her opponent, to enter into the opponent's aggressive energy and turn it against him. If the opponent is going to pull, then let him pull. Do not pull against him; pull in unison with him. Aikido is not waiting for an attack like in jujutsu or judo; aikido is about not being there when the attack comes.

Many historians claim that aikido was influenced by other martial arts most notably aiki-jutsu. But even up to his death Uyeshiba maintained that aikido had no links with any other martial art system.

The aikido instructor has been likened to the eye of a hurricane. In the midst of an attack he is calm and serene, yet perfectly capable of rendering one or more assailants completely helpless. Because of Uyeshiba's pacifist and harmonious attitude, there are no strikes or atemi in aikido.

Only when students are graded to shodan or black belt, can they wear the traditional hakama or black split skirt. When beginning in the art, students usually practise in pairs. The atmosphere is relaxed in the dojo, more so than in most of the other types of martial arts. All the time it is emphasized that peace and harmony must reign. Techniques are divided into standing and sitting ones, with the beginners first learning correct posture, breakfalls and focus.

The world headquarters for aikido is a modern building erected on the site of Uyeshiba's first club in Tokyo. It is known as the Aikikai and presided over by Uyeshiba's son, Kishomaru Uyeshiba.

The mystical power of ki

Without the understanding of the ki in aikido, all the student would ever gain is a series of holds and locks with little or no meaning. Ki is the very essence of the art, but understanding what it is, is another story altogether. In layman's terms it is a source of energy inherent in everyone, a super-power waiting to be tapped and released. This super energy can be defined as mental and spiritual power which is summoned through concentration and breathing techniques. This can then be applied to physical feats. This force of will and energy has no limitations. Even when Uyeshiba was 85 years old he would allow four or five burly black belts to attack him and, by directing his ki, he would throw them around the dojo as if they were rag dolls. Yet Uyeshiba stood only five feet (1.52m) tall and weighed 125 pounds (57 kg).

One of Uyeshiba's top instructors, Koichi Tohei, in a demonstration allowed arrows to be fired at him from a distance of less than 20 feet (6m). He calmly stood there and fended them off with his hands, without one ever touching him.

Morihei Uyeshiba himself once demonstrated that by centring his ki through his stance he became unmoveable. He invited six karate black belts from the audience to see if they could push him over, but heave as they did, all were unsuccessful. At another demonstration Uyeshiba arranged

12 china cups and saucers in a circle, then stood up on the rims of the cups and proceeded to walk around them. Feats such as these defy explanation.

The principle of the ki force is that it moves in circles, and these circles are not limited but expand to infinity. The aikido practitioner is forbidden to use linear motion. Although tremendous power can be generated by linear drive, when used against circular motion it is self-destroying.

As with many of the martial arts, over a period of time the original students of the founding master either become discontented with the way the particular art is going and break away to found their own off-shoot styles, or they feel enough has been learned from the original concept, and leave to expand their own thoughts and ideas on the subject. Aikido is no exception; among the more famous that set up their own styles have been Tomiki and Shioda.

Yoshinkan aikido

The founder of Yoshinkan aikido was Gozo Shioda. Shioda was a student of Uyeshiba. He trained with the great master for 20 years and eventually became his top student. In the early fifties Shioda was invited to the Tokyo police academy to give a demonstration of aikido. He created an instant impression with the police for his skill and was immediately given a 12-month contract to teach them aikido. Shioda then opened his own dojo because there was so much work coming in.

Yoshinkan style is orientated towards actual combat and follows closely the lines of the traditional aiki-jutsu in regard to technique, though spiritually it is still attuned to Uyeshiba's aikido. A very close relationship always existed between Uyeshiba and Shioda, in spite of the latter's break with the existing style.

Tomiki aikido

Tomiki aikido is the only branch of the art that practices competition and tournament fighting. This sporting element was introduced by another of Uyeshiba's disciples, Kenji Tomiki, much against the founder's principle that aikido should be non-competitive. Self-defence is also practised.

Jiu-jitsu

Amongst the many Japanese martial arts, probably the most misrepresented has been jiu-jitsu which is often described as the forerunner of judo and the inspiration for

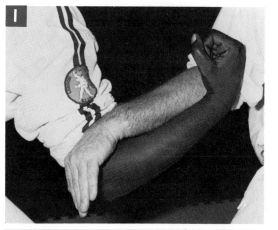

JIU-JITSU

1 *Known as the swan neck, or S block, this lock can break an attacker's arm. Having blocked a punch, the defender instantly snakes his arm over his opponent's, pulling it below shoulder level to reduce its strength.*

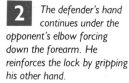

2 *The defender's hand continues under the opponent's elbow forcing down the forearm. He reinforces the lock by gripping his other hand.*

3 *Simply by raising his clasped hands, the defender causes his opponent to experience excruciating pain.*

aikido. Jiu-jitsu in its fullest form was an art of the samurai warrior. Freely translated, jiu-jitsu means the art of gaining victory by yielding or pliancy. In the West it is usually said to mean gentle art. The fighter in this art wins by yielding to strength. The art dates back to antiquity, being known under the various names of tai-jutsu, yawara and hakuda.

There is one legend that was verbally handed down, that relates the story of a Japanese physician who lived in Nagasaki named Akiyama. He had travelled to China to learn new techniques in medicine. While there he learned an art known as hakuda, which consisted of kicking and striking plus seizing and grappling. Akiyama also learned 28 different ways of recovering a man from apparent death. Upon his return to Japan, the doctor began to teach this art to a few selected students, but because he had only a few techniques, his pupils soon got bored and left him. Very much annoyed about this, Akiyama went to the Tenjin shrine for 100 days to meditate and worship. During this period, he is said to have discovered 303 different methods of the art. This multiplication of techniques was brought about because Akiyama had seen a pine tree standing erect in the forest which was broken to pieces during a violent snow storm. Yet a willow tree nearby yielded to the weight of the snow on its branches and did not break. He took this lesson and applied it to the art he had brought from China. He opened another school which was very successful, naming it Yoshin-ryu or willow tree school.

History records that many skills of grappling and throwing abounded in Japan, as long ago as a thousand years. These methods were systematized as jiu-jitsu in 1532 by Hisamori Takenouchi. They formed an integral part of the samurais' training and served as a complement to their more specialized weapon skills. Within this art of jiu-jitsu lay armed as well as unarmed techniques. Use was made of such weapons as the naginata, bo staff and yari (spear). All stressed, as might be expected from skills developed by warriors, maximum effectiveness on the battlefield. Jiu-jitsu is often identified as pure grappling, with the involvement of arm-locks and joint manipulations, but what is perhaps not so well known is that the art also includes kicks and punches. It is thought that these were introduced from the martial arts systems of southern China. Another aspect of jiu-jitsu was that of atemi, the art of attacking pressure points, joints and other vulnerable areas.

Jiu-jitsu is not a contest of muscular strength—in fact this is not a major factor at all. The art relies on balance, leverage and speed to effect the necessary movements, and then available strength is applied to its greatest advantage. Jiu-jitsu tends to wipe out the differences of size, weight, height and reach, thus evening the odds and making the art both acceptable and accessible to women. Female involvement in jiu-jitsu has taken great strides in the last 20 or 30 years to the point that it

Right *Although the practice of jiu-jitsu is normally associated with unarmed self-defence, in fact some exponents also incorporate weapon arts into their training. Here the grandmaster of the Yoshin Ryu, Soke Tsuyoshi Munetoshi Inouye, demonstrates the use of the bo staff against the bokken.*

has begun to show undercurrents of a real social movement. Women's interest in the art stems from wanting to be able to defend themselves, not just from a physical attack but from every kind of intimidation. Jiu-jitsu's modern approach, with its methods of defence and offence without weapons in a personal encounter, nurtures a strong feeling of self-confidence. Through the skills taught in jiu-jitsu, women are now beginning to fight back. Common sense dictates that a woman cannot punch as hard as a man, but jiu-jitsu does not rely on the ability to meet force with force. In most cases the street lout or rapist will be totally ignorant of his would-be victim's specialized knowlege of a martial art such as jiu-jitsu. Before he even attacks, he is already at a disadvantage. Prior knowledge is an essential part of self-defence and constitutes the surprise element that can mean the difference between success and failure. The relatively small limbs and weak muscles of a woman are quite capable of causing total disability to the most powerful man alive, when used with the techniques of jiu-jitsu.

What is jiu-jitsu?

Jiu-jitsu is constantly being confused with the art of judo, although both are distantly related. Jiu-jitsu is far more devastating than its sporting brother judo. Jiu-jitsu is a combination, or series of combinations, of throws, holds and locks applied in most cases upon the limbs. They are carried out in such a manner that by the addition of extra pressure, dislocation of a joint or actual breakage of a bone may occur. The art is based entirely upon a thorough knowledge of body balance, together with an accurate understanding of its construction. The joints of the limbs and body have only limited movement, whether the individual action is backwards, forwards or sideways, or almost rotary. The delicate construction of the joint will not take further movement beyond that limit and if force is exerted, the joint enters the danger area. Further pressure is first met with intense pain and secondly, if the pressure is continued, dislocation of that particular joint. By a carefully thought-out system of holds and locks and the application of leverage, jiu-jitsu supplies the necessary pressure to produce this end result.

At the height of jiu-jitsu's popularity, there were as many as 700 different ryu (schools). The many thousands of techniques in its syllabus aimed at combating every type of attack.

Kuatsu

Kuatsu is the ancient art of resuscitation or revival, itself a branch of jiu-jitsu. It is so highly specialized that years of thorough training were given to instructors who had been carefully selected. They learned the art under a strict oath of secrecy. Kuatsu was considered to be the supreme knowledge in jiu-jitsu. It was customary for those who received the secret knowledge to pay the master a sum of money.

Methods of kuatsu are numerous and vary from school to school. One of the simplest methods used for resuscitating those who have been temporarily suffocated by choking involves grabbing the patient from the back and placing the edge of the palms on the abdomen, pushing upwards in a sharp movement. Groin injuries can be put to rights using methods of kuatsu, although severe blows and strangulations require more complicated methods of recovery. It is thought that the knowledge of kuatsu stems from the sister art of acupuncture, that of shiatsu.

Jiu-jitsu today

It is doubtful that what is practised today bears much resemblance to the art of the feudal samurai. Some of the old schools are

Above Women who take up jiu-jitsu become extremely effective at defending themselves even against armed attackers.

91

SELF-DEFENCE

Jiu-jitsu techniques can often be successfully adapted for use in real-life street situations.

1 A man approaches a girl and asks her the time. While she is momentarily off-guard, he attempts to choke her.

2 The girl slams his ears very hard with her open palms.

3 Then she quickly rakes his face.

4 She follows this up by striking to the side of his ear with her elbow.

5 Then she turns and grabs his sleeve and leg.

6 She bends down sharply, pulling his sleeve with her, so that he loses his balance. He goes over her shoulder and falls to the ground. She can now counter as appropriate, or run away.

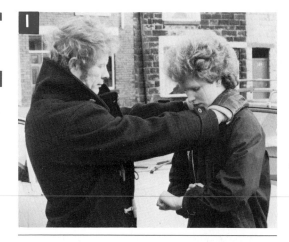

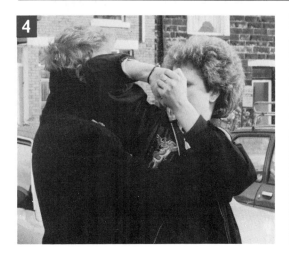

still in existence, practising their art along the traditional lines, but these are very few and far between. The systems today stem mostly from goshin-jutsu, which is a generic name to describe modern jiu-jitsu styles. Goshin-jitsu was perfected at the Kodokan (the supreme authority on judo). Another style that has influenced jiu-jitsu is that of Tenjin Shinyo-ryu, the system of ancient Japan.

Over the last ten years jiu-jitsu has been developed as a sporting and competitive activity. Because of this, many of its lethal techniques have been omitted from training programmes, although at some clubs the dangerous manoeuvres are still taught. Many of today's police forces have used the services of jiu-jitsu instructors to devise part of the training curriculum for police officers. Some of the police arrest and restraint techniques were introduced via army personnel posted overseas, prior to World War II, who had been quick to see the advantages of this Oriental martial art. Almost all the unarmed combat that was learned by special forces during the last war was based upon jiu-jitsu. Indeed, most modern practical self-defence systems in the West are based upon this art.

The birth of judo

Above *A perfect ippon is scored in this middleweight international judo contest, with harai makikomi (sweeping spring hip throw).*

Judo was the brain-child of Dr Jigoro Kano, who established it in 1882 in Tokyo. It is a well-organized system of unarmed techniques, primarily based on throws using leverage and holds. Judo means gentle way. It is not a jitsu art; it is a sporting form partly developed from jiu-jitsu. Outside of China, judo is perhaps the most widely practised of all the martial arts. It can be classed as a sport, a fighting art, a spiritual discipline and an excellent form of physical education. The latter was the primary intention of its founder, who believed that healthy individuals would promote mutual welfare for the ultimate benefit of the nation.

As a youth Kano suffered from ill health and at school he was constantly bullied, so in a concerted effort to combat this he embarked on his own programme of fitness training. Being born after the end of Japan's feudal era, Kano had ample opportunity to sample many of the western world's sports that were being newly introduced to his country. By the time Kano was 17 he decided to study martial arts. Jiu-jitsu looked the obvious choice, so he enrolled under the tutelage of Hachinosuke Fukoda of the Tenjin Shinyo school. This school specialized in atemiwaza or striking techniques and also newaza or grappling methods. The severity of the training took its toll upon Kano, who over a period of time received many injuries. He treated these himself with an odious liquid bought from the village herbalist.

Upon his teacher's death Kano looked around for another school and he joined the Kito Ryu which specialized in nagewaza or throwing techniques. His thirsty mind drank in everything the school had to offer. Then in 1882 Kano founded his own style, to be known as Kano-ryu, but it was later changed to Kodokan judo. Establishing himself at a temple in a poor quarter of Tokyo he began to teach his style to just nine students. During this time he was awarded his master's rank in Kito Ryu jiu-jitsu. A challenge from another school was met, and Kano fought and beat the great champion Fukushima. Because of this the Tenshin Shinyo school also awarded him a master's degree. Kano's name was now beginning to attract attention.

In 1886 the Japanese police force held a grand tournament in which all the jiu-jitsu schools were invited to participate in order to see which of the schools would prevail. With a team of 15 hand-picked judoka the Kodokan judo school won 13 of the 15 matches, thus establishing their supremacy once and for all. Kano's new art was recognized by the Japanese government and also the Butokukwai, the governing body for martial arts.

Today, the world headquarters for all judo is the Kodokan building in Tokyo, but modern sporting judo differs from the traditional judo or Kano jiu-jitsu. As early as World War I judo techniques were being practised in Europe and the oldest club is the Budokwai in London, which was formed in 1918. The British Judo Association was created in 1948 and is the governing body for all judo practised in the UK. It is perhaps interesting to note that the anti-boxing campaign in schools in the early fifties, led by Dr Edith Summerskill, helped to get judo off the ground. By 1958 judo had become acceptable as a physical activity in schools. In 1952 an international judo organization was established, to promote competition at world level. It was named the International Judo Federation

JUDO

1 Fifth dan World Middleweight Champion (1981) Neil Adams prepares to demonstrate his right (migi) body drop (taiotoshi) on fellow international Ray Stevens. He steps around and back with his left foot, having grasped his opponent's jacket in both hands.

2 He pulls out with his left hand and pushes up with his right, meanwhile bending his left knee. This breaks his opponent's balance. He then steps across and alongside his opponent's right foot.

3 By snapping the right leg straight and pulling down with the left arm while continuing to push with the right, the opponent is forced up and forwards.

4 The drop is achieved and the opponent thrown to the floor.

Right *International player Roy Inman is seen practising at the Budokwai judo club. He uses kosotougakae (minor outer breaking throw) to take his opponent to the mat. Club members in the background await their turn.*

(IJF) and comprises over 70 member nations. In the Tokyo Olympics of 1964 judo was introduced as the first Oriental martial way. Thus, the West had accepted Kano's judo with open arms, as a physical, educational and sporting pursuit.

Judo the art

Judo is now practised in almost every country in the world. Judo techniques are divided into three categories: tachiwaza (standing techniques), newaza (ground techniques) and atemiwaza (vital point techniques). Within these three categories are many sub-divisions that encompass the whole periphery of judo technique. Tachiwaza is also known as nagewaza (throwing techniques). Atemiwaza, derived from jiu-jitsu, is practised only for self-defence and is prohibited in competition.

In a judo match, usually one point is needed to defeat an opponent. The points can be gained from any number of techniques: for a clean throw, for controlling an opponent on the ground for 30 seconds, or for obtaining a surrender or submission by applying either a stranglehold or an arm-lock. If neither opponent obtains a point in the given time, the referee can make an award for aggressiveness, otherwise termed good fighting spirit.

Similar to karate, the judo grading is based upon both proficiency in contest and on knowledge of the art. Differentiations in rank are shown by the coloured belts worn by the judoka. Beginners start with a white belt and graduate to yellow, orange, green, blue, and then brown belt. Ultimately, the student advances to shodan or first degree black belt. The dan grades range from first dan to tenth dan. Although it is possible to attain a 12th dan, no one has actually ever achieved this rank, save for the founder Jigoro Kano.

To practise judo the student wears a uniform of white with a kimono-style top and trousers, referred to as a judogi. A class observes the formal etiquette, which involves bowing before entering and leaving the dojo and also bowing to one's instructor or sensei. A bow is also exchanged between judoka at the beginning and end of each practice session.

Randori

About 70 to 80 per cent of judo training consists of randori or free sparring, in which two contestants practise throwing and grappling under the conditions of actual contest. Randori is usually two judoka attacking and defending at will. Although this practice is an all-out effort

95

Above Sixth dan Brian Jacks demonstrates to a class of juniors the importance of low hips in hold-downs and legs spread wide apart to control the opponent.

by each participant to out-do the other, it can be modified to meet specific needs. For example, most instructors encourage beginner students to yield rather than resist. For the judo competitor, randori practice is an unavoidable necessity. It is the most valuable of all judo practice methods. The judoka cannot be properly prepared for a tournament or competition without going out on the mat and grappling with other skilled sparring partners. Indeed, beginners are encouraged to ask the higher grades for practice, thus gaining good experience. The establishment of patterns of attack and the improvement in timing may be of use not only in competition but also in self-defence situations. Combatants may use whatever methods they like, provided they do not hurt each other and obey the rules of judo etiquette. Popular opinion seems to be that randori is pre-arranged sparring. It is not. Randori consists of spontaneous free-fighting, but under controlled conditions.

Randori relies quite a lot upon the play of emotions and the exertion of will. Many psychological factors are involved. Attempting to up-end an adversary while at the same time defending against attacks can be a very frustrating experience. Needless to say, during randori the judoka should not talk or let his or her mind wander to other things. Over 50 years ago, the founder Kano once stated that mental training in judo can be done as well in randori as it can in kata.

Speed in randori is absolutely essential, both in mind and action, and this is part of the training. Unless one decides quickly and acts promptly the opportunity either in attacking or defending will be lost. Both judoka should always be alert and constantly looking for the weak points in the other, ready to attack whenever the opportunity allows.

Left Groundwork practice plays an important part in judo. International competitors Karen Briggs and Sharron Rendle are seen here in a training session.

Below A well-balanced judoka should be as competent in grappling techniques (newaza) as in throwing (tachiwaza). Here a class practises holds and armlocks.

Shorinji kempo

Shorinji kempo has often been described as a mixture of karate and aikido, though this is somewhat of an enigma. This art as practised in Japan has a quasi-religious aspect about it, being greatly influenced by the Buddhist sect of Kongo Zen. The word kongo means diamond and Zen is the school of Bodhidharma. The followers of Kongo Zen believe that the only power people should be guided by is knowledge of the world, and that a belief in one god simply divests man of most of his moral responsibility. Practice of this martial art in the West rests mainly on the philosophy and applied techniques, rather than adherence to religious principles.

Shorinji is the Japanese translation of the Chinese word Shaolin-su, and kempo is the Japanese translation of the Chinese word chuan-fa meaning way of the fist. Although essentially a modern Japanese martial art its roots go back to the kung fu of the Shaolin temple in northern China. The guiding light behind the art's introduction to Japan was Doshin So. Doshin So was born in the Okayaman prefecture in 1911. While still very young his father died and he was sent to live with his grandfather in Manchuria. Twelve years later his grandfather, an employee on the railroads, died and he was forced to return to Japan under the patronage of a certain Mr Mitsuru Toyama who is credited with founding the secret society known as the Black Dragon (Amur River Society), and had been a very good friend of Doshin So's late grandfather. In the late 1920s Japan became heavily involved in the politics of the Asian mainland, specifically China. Because of Doshin So's invaluable knowledge of Manchuria gleaned during his formative years while living with his grandfather, he was sent back as a secret agent under the auspices of the Black Dragon Society which held loyalties to the Japanese government. To facilitate his covert activities he became a disciple of a Taoist priest named master Chin Ryo. This priest was a section chief of a secret society known as Zaijari which had off-shoots into the infamous Triads. During Doshin So's travels across China with master Chin Ryo, he discovered that his mentor was also a master of a little-known style of kung fu called Byakuremonken, which was a branch of kempo originally developed at the Shaolin temple. Eagerly the young disciple learned all he could from the old priest. Doshin So gradually began to build up various types of techniques, culling from the individual endeavours of the many kempo masters he met on his journey. By far the biggest influence on the Shorinji system was Doshin So's meeting in Peking with the 20th headmaster of the northern Shaolin (Shorinji) Giwamonken school of kempo. Instantly he attached himself as a disciple to this new master, Bunta So.

The next few years were spent studying hard all the principles behind the Giwa-monken system, until eventually upon mastery of the style he was bestowed with the great honour of the 21st headmastership of the Shorinji school. Over the next 10 years Doshin So developed the techniques of the Giwamonken and Byakuremonken schools adding his own interpretations to the various bits and pieces he had picked up from the other masters of kempo in his youth.

In 1945 the Russian army entered Man-churia and Doshin So as a Japanese national had to beat a hasty retreat. Aided by secret society members he escaped and finally emerged in his homeland a year later. The devastation he saw in Japan in those post-war years saddened him greatly. Deter-mined to rebuild the morale and national pride of Japan's youth he set upon a crusade almost single-handedly to restore those lost values by founding a Chinese Shaolin temple on Japanese soil, injecting into his movement philosophy, religion, moral obligation and a belief in one's own ability to overcome any obstacle. The site chosen for this venture was the harbour town of Tadotsu on Shikoku. Black mar-keteering was rife; virtually the whole economy was run by the Yakuza (gangs-ters). He found a group of followers and trained them in martial arts. When this small band were deemed competent they set about cleaning up the town. The US occupying forces had banned weapons of all kinds, and firearms anyway were totally non-existent, so armed with their empty hands and martial arts knowledge, the first Shorinji students took on the mighty Yaku-za. Within 18 months Tadotsu was freed from the Yakuza stranglehold. The town's youth were greatly enthused by what a small band of dedicated martial artists had accomplished, and quickly flocked to join the organization.

Doshin So established the world head-quarters for Shorinji kempo on the out-skirts of Tadotsu. The order is kept deliber-ately religious so that students never lose sight of the original aim, the teachings of Buddha. Shorinji fighting is looked upon as a vehicle with which to foster self-development and philosophical under-standing, ultimately leading to an even greater understanding of mind and body, thereby transforming students into more balanced people.

The founder Doshin So uttered a slogan for Shorinji that all students are expected to live by, which is 'Live half for yourself and half for others.' As the martial art of Shorinji kempo grew, Doshin So began to realize his dream of universal brotherhood. His religious philosophies became more and more profound and he issued such precepts as, 'Work harder from this day onwards to build a happy and peaceful society.' In the dark days of post-war Japan, when a sense of aimlessness pre-vailed, he decided to offer a helping hand. The young flocked to the town of Tadotsu to join the ranks of multiplying Shorinji students. Within 10 years Doshin So had more than a million members in his orga-nization in Japan alone. He registered his art with the government as a religion.

The uniqueness of Shorinji kempo lies in the fact that it does not just preach a way of life but incorporates all its teachings into direct experience, with the aim of produc-ing a balanced human being in harmony with others. It is perhaps interesting to note that as an empty-hand martial system, Shorinji kempo has no structure for weapon training, except for a long wooden pole or staff. This is because the art was originally designed for the use of Buddhist priests, so it cannot condone the use of swords, spears, or any other weapons.

The techniques of the Shorinji kempo system

The fighting techniques of the Shorinji system comprise both soft and hard move-ments. The 700 or so techniques are said to cover every possible means of defending

Right A Shorinji kempo master demonstrates his skills in combat with two assailants. He first disarms one, before defending himself against another attacker.

and protecting oneself in almost any situation. Since the techniques of kempo are not determined by strength or size, but by scientific application, persons of either sex or any age can effectively defend themselves.

Shorinji kempo techniques are based firstly upon defence; attack is the last resort. The most important principle in the fighting system is the application of pressure to the vital points of the human body. This knowledge was liberally gleaned from ancient Chinese medical treatises. Shorinji designates 142 vital points on the human body, where a practitioner can cause damage or inflict severe pain. Throughout training, the principles of Kongo Zen and its disciplines are strictly adhered to. Much emphasis is placed upon training with a partner and through mutual experience identifying with one another the pain thresholds implied by the techniques. This avoids permanently injuring a fellow student, and at the same time, in following the edicts of Kongo Zen, a mutual trust and empathy with each other is developed. An interesting practice for the health is implemented at the end of every training session, called seiho. This is a method of regulating the circulation, the nervous system and bone stress. Through severe training methods and strenuous exercising a build-up of lactic acid occurs in the body. By observing the seiho principle, which in effect is a kind of massage, the acid accumulation is relieved, tension is lessened, and new energy restored, thereby promoting health for future endeavours.

The badge that practitioners of Shorinji kempo wear on their uniforms is that of the manji. It is an ancient symbol, often found on ruined temples, representing the cyclic progression of the cosmos. Doshin So adopted the symbol as he felt it expressed visually the philosophy of Kongo Zen. In fact it consists of two forms symbolizing the unity of opposites: one (the Nazi sign) emphasizes power, the other (with the arms facing the other way) love.

The religious aspects of Shorinji kempo are perhaps not as strictly adhered to here in the West, although the philosophy and Za-zen (seated meditation) are observed. Doshin So passed away His daughter is now head of Shorinji kempo.

Sumo wrestling

Above Sumo wrestling still *follows the time-honoured Japanese traditions depicted in this print by Kunisada.*

Wrestling and grappling arts are probably the oldest known form of unarmed fighting in existence. Every country has a heritage of unarmed grappling methods, but nowhere in the world is there a wrestling system that quite matches that of Japan's sumo men. This strictly indigenous art or sport is quite unique to Japan. Steeped in Shintoism, it is part fighting and part ritualistic ceremony.

Sumo wrestlers, or to give them their proper term sumotori, fight unarmed and almost naked, save for a heavy loincloth type of garment known as a mawashi. The mawashi consists of a heavy piece of silk ten yards long and two feet wide (9 x ·6m). It is folded into four and then wrapped around the waist and groin, to resemble a gigantic baby's nappy. The area in which the sumotori fight is called a dohyo. This is a dirt mound covered in sand measuring fifteen feet (4.5m) in diameter. The object of the sport is incredibly simple: one wrestler has either to eject his opponent from this ring (unroped) or down him inside it. In the former case he wins if any part of his opponent's body, touches down outside this area; in the latter if any part of the body above the knee hits the dust. The methods a sumotori uses in applying this task involve throwing, pushing, tripping and even pulling.

When a match begins both fighters carry out a ritual ceremony from their respective corners which can take up to half an hour to perform. This involves scattering salt in the ring to purify it. Because of the deep Shinto interest, a priest is always on hand to officiate. Indeed, many of the more important bouts actually take place at Shinto shrines. The salt purifying ceremony must take at least four minutes to perform, and the wrestler is judged by the audience upon how well he does this. Then the two sumotori assume a crouching position, and at the referee's signal charge at each other, meeting in the centre of the ring with a squelching smack. This initial charge is called tachiai, and is thought to be the moment of truth in sumo.

The actual fights are amazingly brief, the majority being over in less than a minute. In fact some matches have lasted only about five seconds. Neither wrestler has any right to protest, the decision of the referee being final. Draws never occur either; in the event of a tie another match is ordered. Strength and stability being the prime requisites, it is not surprising to see the average sumotori tipping the scales at 350 pounds (158kg) plus. Most of this tremendous weight is concentrated in the lower part of the body, which is gained by following a diet of very rich food, combined with special exercises. The aim of this is to produce the characteristic thick legs, heavy hips and large protruding stomach, which in turn create a low centre of gravity giving good balance and stability to the sumo man. The secret of becoming a good fighter is said to be in the legs and hips. Because of this, much training is involved in strengthening these two areas.

Professional sumo is divided into six divisions, which are further subdivided into ranks. These classifications, however, have nothing to do with weight. Advancement up the ladder of success is based solely on skill.

The origins of sumo

Japanese sumo wrestling is thought by some to be more than 2,000 years old. Its origins lie in a mixture of folklore and myth. Japan's oldest literary document, the *Kojiki* (records of ancient matters) penned in the early 700s, states that the gods fought for possession of the land. An ensuing bare-handed battle between the two deities resulted in the god Takemika-zuchi winning. Although little credence can be given to this fanciful tale, it does demonstrate that the early Japanese settled disputes through hand-to-hand combat methods (as did other ancient societies elsewhere), and that the outcome was interpreted as 'divine will'. Such conclusions would have been drawn by the Shinto priests of the time, hence the close connection between combat and religion right from the start.

Another sumo legend records the great battle between Kuyehaya and Sakune. Apparently a huge giant of a man named Kuyehaya had been bragging that if anyone were to search the world, they would never find anyone to compare with him in strength. It was rumoured that he could straighten hooks with his bare hands and break the horns off cattle. The Emperor asked for someone to come forward and contest the braggart's claims. A man named Sakune offered his services and the great duel began. Stamping their feet hard on the ground the two men stood opposite one another. Kuyehaya began by kicking his opponent in the ribs and breaking them. Sakune retaliated with a devastating kick to the groin, completely smashing the area and killing him. That particular fight is credited as being the first sumo match in Japan between mortals. Today that first fight is honoured by staging a big sumo event on 7 July every year, at the place it occurred.

In 1684 official sanction was given to kanjin-zumo (sumo) and it became a professional martial art and sport. A series of rules and regulations were drawn up and supervisors were employed to see that they were carried out. Every town and village in Japan boasted at least one professional sumotori. The greatest of the sumo men were given samurai status by the feudal lords. A hundred years later sumo became a national sport. When Commodore Matthew Perry arrived in Japan with his 'black ships' in 1853, line upon line of huge sumo wrestlers were assembled on the beach to indicate to the westerners the size and strength of the Japanese nation.

When Japan entered the modern era, sumo for a while fell into a decline. The sumotori gained employment as bodyguards to rich merchants and also guarded the doors of the brothels in the Yoshiwara (the red-light district). In 1889 a man named Takasago petitioned for the reinstatement of sumo wrestling as a sport. Realizing great success, the Tokyo Ozumo Kyokai was born (Tokyo Sumo Association). The complete recovery of sumo as a national sport in Japan came upon the completion of the Kokugikan, the hall of national sport. Today the art is controlled by the Japan Sumo Association.

The highest award a sumo wrestler can receive is the Emperor's Cup. This was first given in 1926 to the grand champion Tsunenohana.

Sumo Facts

Although strictly speaking only Japanese-born people can become sumotori, one westerner, Hawaiian born Jesse Kahualua, did break through the barriers of this thousand-year-old tradition. Fighting under the name of Takamiyama, he climbed to the top of the tree to become grand champion or yokozuna.

Once in the yokozuna category, a wrestler must be able to continually demonstrate his superiority. The unwritten code of the yokozuna is that he will retire voluntarily if he loses more than eight consecutive shobu (bouts).

The sumotori are not permitted to wear the familiar top-knot hair style until they reach the maku-uchi division, which is one of the top two categories on the sumo scale. The sumo men never dress their own hair; this is left to a special hairdresser employed by the particular sumo stable. A sumotori's hair is never cut until he retires. When he does eventually stand down, a special ceremony takes place called danpatsu-shiki. This is the ritual of cutting a lock of hair from the wrestler, usually peformed by his associates and patrons.

A fighter always begins a contest by stamping his feet. This is to drive away all the evil spirits in the ring. All sumotori are very superstitious.

The Japanese word for a sumo tournament is basho.

Right *Foremost exponent of ninjutsu in the West is American Stephen Hayes. He personally has helped to promote interest in this ancient art of stealth to the point where its popularity is gaining ground at a tremendous rate. In his opinion it is 'the ultimate combat system'. Many weapons are employed in the art, including this sword.*

THE NINJA

'A single false move loses the game.'

During a period long ago there emerged in Japan a superb group of warriors whose skills were classed as being almost magical. These were the legendary ninja, the warriors of darkness, assassins of the night. Ninja training was designed to produce the complete fighting man. The art of ninjutsu wreaked death and havoc among the enemy, instilling fear into the local community, until the very name, ninja, would send a cold shiver of doom down the spine. Feared throughout the land, the shadow warriors became legends in their own time.

The art of war
Just over 2,000 years ago a Chinese scholar wrote a treatise entitled *The Art Of War*; his name was Sun Tzu. This book covered every aspect of waging war, in particular the strategy employed. Sun Tzu stated, 'The skilful strategist should be able to subdue the enemy's army without engaging it, to take his cities without laying siege to them, and to overthrow his state without bloodying swords.' Sun Tzu was convinced that careful planning based upon sound information of the enemy would contribute to a speedy victory. Furthermore, the use of espionage behind the enemy lines could shorten a military campaign tremendously. Using spies for subversive ends, including assassinations of military leaders, could, in some cases, even prevent actual hostilities breaking out. Sun Tzu never conceived war in terms of mass slaughter and destruction. This brilliant military classic became an indispensable handbook for the Chinese warlords of the period, *c.* 500 BC.

The art of stealth
In the sixth century dissidents from China began to arrive in Japan seeking sanctuary. With them came the book written by Sun Tzu. Chinese Buddhism was already beginning to thrive in Japan and so the great books of learning from China were avidly studied by the young Japanese priests. About this time a battle for succession to the throne was being waged by the Prince Regent Shotoku. It was he, on the advice of the priests, who first engaged men to spy and bring back information on his rivals. When Shotoku, a fervent Buddhist, finally became ruler he promulgated the religion. Upon his death 30 years later, the Japanese became embroiled in a bitter struggle over which doctrine should be designated as the state religion—either Shintoism or Buddhism.

At this time a warrior priest (yamabushi) came forward to try to solve the dispute by promoting a different form of Buddhism called Shugendo. This Shugendo quickly became very popular and the aristocracy feared that unless the yamabushi was stopped he would rapidly gain power. So a large army was sent out to defeat him and his followers. Overpowering odds won the day and the yamabushi together with a few disciples fled to the mountains of Iga for refuge. Iga was a vast desolate area where few people ever travelled. The forests were shrouded in mists and the mountain paths were barely accessible. It was in this region that the art of ninjutsu began.

The ninja clans
For the next 400 years the warrior mountain priests lived and worked in this desolate area. They raised families and studied the teachings and philosophies of Buddhism, also learning the secret knowledge known as mikkyo. Mikkyo constituted the teachings of occultism and occult-based practices of the Buddhist sect of Shingon, meaning 'true words'. It involved the worship of nature spirits and other mystic teachings. Shingon was also heavily influenced by Tantric beliefs. Here, in virtual

isolation, these ascetic warrior priests studied nature and the elements, chanting special incantations in an effort to unlock the secrets of the universe and the mind. Over several centuries their theories of the occult were developed for the purpose of uniting human mental powers with supernatural forces. Through the influence of Tantrism many yoga systems and principles were followed. A method was devised for concentrating all the will and energy into one endeavour at any given time. This superior kind of power was summoned by the adepts, who employed hand signs involving intricate finger-knitting patterns, and then in a trance-like state, concentrated all their energies upon these patterns. The various hand patterns were known as the five manifestations; earth, fire, wind, water and void. Once the mind had been settled, a trance-like state overcame the practitioner, inducing physiological changes that included a slowing-down of blood pressure and heart beat. An experienced ninja could change his inhalations and exhalations to such an extent that he could 'shallow breathe', which, as we shall see, aided the ninja in faking his own death.

These finger-entwining hand patterns were informally referred to as kuji-in (energy channelling). There are 81 such hand positions, able to cover every circumstance that the ninja might find himself in. It is thought that because of the ninja's early isolation, the long meditative practices and mystical teachings, they developed their inherent powers of psychic perception. Also, through increased sensitivity they were able to attune their mental awareness beyond the usual five senses. Such capabilities played upon the imaginations of the superstitious feudal peasants. Stories abounded of how a slain ninja could return to life or of how he could walk through solid walls, disappear at will, walk on water, or change into a bird and fly away. Even the educated samurai were impressed by this invisible enemy.

The training begins

In Japan's history the Kamakura Period (1192-1333) became known as the golden age of ninjutsu. The constant conflicts between lords and court officials vying for power, together with general political unrest, provided the perfect setting for the talents of the ninja. As these mountain-dwelling experts in death and mayhem began to emerge from their strongholds, there were plenty of influential people ready to employ their unique skills.

Many schools of ninjutsu began to spring up in the areas around Iga and Koga. Exponents of the art were born and trained within the family clan, each ryu (school) characterized by its own particular brand of espionage. The clans began to grow, until over 70 distinct schools blossomed. Absolute secrecy was the foundation upon which all ninja clans depended. The rigid security precautions included their code of dying rather than, for instance, divulging information concerning their base camp, and this was strictly enforced.

To maintain the secrecy of the ninja tradition further, three divisions were established to form a type of pecking order. At the top was the jonin, the high-ranking administrator, whose job it was to meet the war-lord or government official who wanted to hire the services of the ninja. The jonin was also responsible for running his particular clan and giving the orders. The next stage was the rank of chunin, the middle-man or go-between. His duties included setting up training programmes and passing the orders down to the field agent, the person who would actually carry out the mission. This agent was known in the hierarchy as the genin. It was the genin and his exploits that made ninja feared throughout the land.

The ninja's training began at birth. Barely able to walk, he would learn simple children's games that had ulterior motives. Before the child was five years old he

Left *This is a popular print from the Tokugawa period showing a ninja making a secret finger sign.*

104

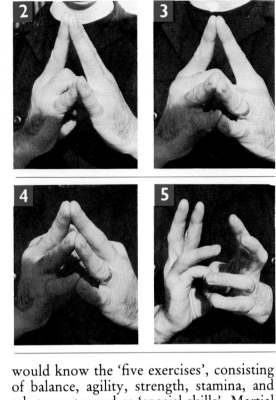

NINJUTSU

There are five attitudes in ninjutsu represented by the secret finger signs shown above (from left to right): earth, water, fire, wind and void (unseen). Each attitude should induce a state of mind to provide a foundation for technique. For instance, fire is aggressive and fast moving, it climbs and is inclined towards weapons. On the other hand water is flowing, symbolizing a continuous method of defeating an opponent. By forming and concentrating on these hand signs, the ninja is able to adopt the best frame of mind for any particular venture.

would know the 'five exercises', consisting of balance, agility, strength, stamina, and what was termed as 'special skills'. Martial arts training was given almost immediately with weapons such as the bo staff, sword, kyu (the bow and arrow), shuriken (a star-shaped throwing implement), and other special weapons identified with ninjutsu. The unarmed combat method of tai-jitsu was practised arduously. Before the age of seven, a ninja child would have been taught how to hold his breath under water for long periods, how to endure the rigours of inclement weather, to climb trees and cliff faces, scale walls, survive for days without food and drink, learn to sleep on a tree branch without falling off, and dislocate his young limbs at will. This latter exercise would aid the ninja to escape, in later life, if he was ever captured and bound. As the ninja child grew up, his life would be one long training programme. The simple nursery games would take on a deadly serious aspect, and the arts he was learning would be honed to perfection. As his youthful understanding grew, so too did the subject matter he was expected to embrace. He was taught always to expect the unexpected and he was schooled in psychology, so that when on a mission, whether it was to assassinate or purely spy for information, he could play on people's egos and use flattery and deception as formidable weapons.

Methods of training

The myriad skills the ninja had to learn before he was able to go out on a mission would seem to take half a lifetime to learn. But the ninja knew no other kind of existence, and isolated in the mountains he had any amount of time to acquire these skills.

The balancing exercises began by walking across thin tree branches. From there the young ninja would progress on to a thin wooden beam, usually stretched across a stream. He would be taught to run along it, jump and turn around, fight on it, even sleep on it, and all without losing his balance. As his skills grew, the beam would be raised higher and thorns scattered underneath. In this way the young ninja knew that if he fell, he would be badly pricked by the thorns. This gave him the added incentive to tread warily, using all his powers of balance and mental concentration. The trainee repeated this exercise until the beam was replaced by a log across a mountain ravine. Still the exercises continued until he eventually lost all fear of great heights and could run across a tightrope like at circus performer.

Stamina training was deemed essential for the ninja. Although he was a very able horseman, out in the field it was not always possible to find such transport and generally it was only the rich lords who had horses. So a ninja had to be able to run great distances in a short amount of time, especially if he were carrying important intelligence back to his superiors. To facilitate this the ninja students ran distances of two and three miles at a time, as fast as they possibly could. Month after month the distance was kept the same and they just concentrated upon gaining speed at every run. The teachers would place a light straw mat against the runner's chest, kept in place by the force of the wind. This indicated to the runner that he was maintaining the required speed. Should the mat fall, the student knew he was below par with his speed. Gradually the three miles would be increased to six, and then to twelve and so on, until a fully trained ninja ready for the field could cover distances of 50 miles or more at lightning pace.

All ninja had to possess maximum strength and training for this came very early on in life. One method used was for the trainee to hang suspended from the bough of a tree for hours on end. This not only developed his arm strength but also served as a mental endurance exercise as well. In hanging there, the ninja overcame his threshold of pain. This also enabled him to practise remaining motionless hidden amid the branches. This in later life could perhaps aid him in eluding pursuers, or even in preparing an ambush.

While the child ninja's bones and tendons were pliable, he was taught how to manipulate them and contort his joints, so that he could dislocate parts of his body at will. This skill was especially useful for gaining entry into the smallest of castle windows and for freeing himself of ropes if he was ever captured. Even chains could be cast loose, which all added to the legend that these men were superhuman and could not be bound and captured. If a samurai ever managed to employ his skills of jiu-jitsu in a hand-to-hand combat with a ninja, a wrist or arm-lock could be quickly evaded by the ninja, giving him the opportunity to counter-attack.

As the ninja child grew up he became a perfectionist in everything connected with his ultimate survival in the field. In short, he was a super athlete, devastating fighting machine, sharp-witted con-man, and an expert pharmacist and actor. The ninja was able to master many disguises and he could adopt the pose and skills of a priest, beggar, farmer or merchant. If he were assigned an assassination target, he adopted the social mannerisms of the class of person he was designated to kill. This made it easier for him to merge in with that particular person's walk of life and therefore to get nearer to him. If the ninja was out just to gather information, he would mingle with the people of that specific region, dressed perhaps as a wandering priest or a travelling merchant, listening to any careless word that may be spoken. With a combination of deceptive ruses and good psychology, he would glean information from likely sources by catering to the informants' egos, praising their looks or social standing, or even promising huge amounts of money. So clever at assuming other identities, the ninja could, if discovery seemed imminent, actually perform the duties of the particular class of person he was disguised as. He could sing and dance, conduct religious ceremonies, or discuss the latest farming prices.

History has recorded that a famous ninja named Momochi Sandayu, in order to maintain complete anonymity, kept three different homes each with his own wife and family. Sandayu, who was an Iga ninja, adopted three entirely different lifestyles for each home. This way he could operate in one area, and then, if discovery seemed likely, he would disappear and emerge 50 miles away as another person, complete with home, wife and family.

Ninja field tactics

Even after the long years of training, the ninja were deemed expendable by the chunin and jonin. So it was therefore in the ninja's own hands whether or not he survived on a mission. If the ninja by chance was captured by his enemy while performing his task, he could be assured that he would be tortured mercilessly and put to death very slowly. The captured ninja would have to follow his iron-clad code of discipline not to talk. The ninja was sworn to secrecy on the tactics of his arts and the whereabouts of the ninja strongholds. He did not dare to divulge any of this information to the enemy, and would preferably try to commit suicide. Any ninja who was disloyal was ruthlessly hunted down by other members of his clan and put to death. In fact if a small band of ninja was operating in an area and it looked as if one of them might be caught, he would be killed instantly by his own associates before they made good their own escape.

The ninja travelling fast and light to his allocated destination could only carry a limited amount of supplies and equipment, the bulk of which consisted of his weapons. So it was necessary for him to live off the land he travelled over. His years of training in the wilderness had taught him to identify herbs and plants as potential remedies and also as food. The ninja's surroundings, wherever he may be, were his home, his food and medicine cabinet. Everything in nature was useful to him and his knowledge of survival, no matter what the terrain, helped him to deal with every situation. The field agent knew that survival was a state of mind. In the depths of winter, travelling across the wild open spaces with snow and ice all around and freezing winds biting into the flesh, many a lesser person would have given up. But not the ninja. No matter how barren and bleak his predicament may have looked, through bringing into focus the powerful force of his mind and concentrating it on a given problem, he could quickly assess the right action to take in order to stay alive. He knew that survival entailed effective operation in all seasons. In the winter, his customary black outfit was reversed to become white, making him virtually invisible amid the snow. Even the elements had their uses; the long sharply pointed icicles could be snapped off and employed to kill some unwary castle guard standing alone on sentry duty.

The ninja always planned ahead, knowing that for each situation he prepared for, there would always be a dozen others he

Above *Learning how to move without being seen is an important part of ninjutsu training. Here students practise crawling in the snow.*

Right *The ninja warrior could gain access to anywhere by utilizing climbing skills learned and practised from birth.*

could never foresee. If he were on a mission hundreds of miles away from his own area, he would not know what facilities were available to him. Because of this, everything he carried upon his persons had to have a dual purpose. His sword, which was much shorter than a samurai's, was a veritable box of tricks. The scabbard was longer than the blade by about three inches (7.5 cm) or so. This enabled him to store poisons, powdered medicines and blinding powders in its detachable bottom. If he was pursued by enemy soldiers he could remove this lower piece, dive into a lake or river and use the hollow scabbard to breath through. Tricks such as this all added to the

illusion that the ninja could disappear at will without a trace. The long cord that strapped the sword to his back could be used for climbing, or for tying someone up, or even employed for snaring small game. His special costume, called a shinobi sho-zoku, consisted of jacket, trousers, hood, and shoes which were split-toed. Within this garb were many pockets and pouches, in which he could carry all manner of useful items to aid him on his mission or in his escape. A small straw mat was usually upon his person. This could be placed over his face and held in position with his scarf-like hood. Thus attired, he could enter a smoke-filled building, or likewise escape from one without being suffocated by the fumes. The split toes of his tabi (shoes) helped him to climb fortifications, to gain access to an intended victim.

Alone in the wilds, the ninja lived on a day-to-day basis. His refuge varied according to whatever was available. If time and conditions allowed, he would make himself a dug-out shelter, lined with leaves for warmth and roofed with tree bark held together with coarse grass. Another method was to burrow into the side of a small hill and sleep in the recess, covering the front with an uprooted bush.

The woods and fields were a ninja's kitchen, but if he knew beforehand that the terrain he would be travelling across was particularly bleak and inhospitable, he could take a small light package of easy-to-carry rations that would help sustain him until other food could be found. Bearing in mind that through his rugged childhood training, the ninja learned to survive on the minimum amount of sustenance, his rations might include ground fihbones, which are particularly high in vitamin C, and the Japanese wild radish called daikon, which provided a source of vitamin A, thus preventing night blindness. The ninja where possible had to maintain a balanced diet to survive in the wilds. An expert in nutrition, he would be wary of heavy foods such as greasy or oily meat products, which, taking a long time to digest, had the effect of making the body sluggish and tired. He knew that the feeling of lethargy could impair judgement and mental awareness. So it wasn't just a matter of a ninja eating anything available. It had to be conducive to aiding his performance in the field. A particular food he carried with him was a kind of 'K' ration; this was a substance made from soya beans called tofu. Tofu is easily digested, low in fat and helps the body make protein in a direct and efficient manner. One problem arose concerning the ninja's eating habits, that he had to pay particular attention to, and that was building a fire. In the less populated areas, where a wisp of smoke could be spotted for miles around, he had to be satisfied with eating very little cooked food.

The winter months, spent out in the open with no fire for warmth, might seem like an open invitation to death, but once again the mystical powers the ninja had learned as a child came into play. Through meditation and concentration, the ninja became one with his environment; he generated his warmth from within and survived the cold.

Poisons and medicines

The ninja alone on a mission had to be his own doctor and pharmacologist. Nature's curatives abounded all around him and he was expert enough to know which plants and roots could heal him. Fungi and edible mushrooms were ready available almost everywhere. Depending upon the species, they had multiple uses. Some fungi contain natural antibiotics and these were used for healing open sword wounds. Other types were boiled and pounded and then administered as hallucinatory drugs to the enemy, as a means of persuading them to betray secrets. Certain others contained a deadly poisonous alkaloid that once assimilated could kill immediately. This was useful when the ninja was sent out to

Right *A varied assortment of ninja weapons including swords (katana), sai and climbing claws. In the ninja's hand are the shuriken used for throwing at a victim, or for creating a distraction. When tipped with poison, the spikes could cause instant death.*

confuse and disorientate the enemy army, ahead of his own employer's forces. The ninja, disguised as a cook, could infiltrate the lines and virtually wipe out the enemy force single-handed, without a blow being levelled. This skilful strategy was in line with Sun Tzu's ideas contained in his book on warfare.

Another poison that was used for centuries by the ninja, was that of the fugu fish, commonly known as the blow fish, which is indigenous to Japan. The poison in this fish is particularly virulent. A mere eight milligrams can effect an almost instantaneous death by attacking part of the brain, completely paralyzing the muscles related to breathing. Even today in Japan this fish, which is deemed a delicacy, is served in specially licensed restaurants, but obviously the poison organs are removed first. All it took to gain the demise of an intended victim, was for the ninja to disguise himself as a servant and serve a piece of the raw fish organ on a plate, hidden among other raw fish morsels. One mouthful was all that was needed.

The weapons of the ninja

In the practice of his trade the ninja was expected to master an awesome array of weapons, one of which was called a kusari-kama. This consisted of a strong link chain with a weight at one end and a razor-sharp sickle at the other. It could be fastened around the ninja's waist and carried easily, but should it be needed in a hurry it could be ready for action in a split second. He would swirl it around his head and either release it to ensnare his victim, or twirl the weighted end around his enemy's limbs and then finish him off with the blade. This weapon was modelled on an earlier weapon called kyoketsu shoge. This was similar, but instead of the chain it was made from knotted animal hair or cord. It had a large metal ring at one end and a sickle-shaped blade at the other, with a second dagger-like blade protruding outwards. Many of the weapons used were specialized, such as the tetsu-bishi or caltrop. The barbs looked very similar to those on barbed wire, or closely resembling the 'jacks' from the children's game of the same name. These would be scattered around a ninja's route of escape, so that when his pursuers gave chase they would tread on the sharp points and fall down in pain. It was not unknown for ninjas to coat the spikes with poison for even more devastating results.

The ninja bo staff was not simply a six-foot (1.8m) bamboo pole, as used in

1 *These climbing claws had many uses, from scaling castle walls to climbing trees, providing the wearer with the abilities of a cat.*

2 *Their lethal spikes could also be employed as a weapon, for instance by raking an opponent's face.*

with a sudden pull from the bo staff. His legs entangled in the chain, the samurai would fall to the ground to be suddenly leapt upon by the ninja, who by this time would have pulled out a short knife concealed in the other end of the bo staff, and plunged it into the helpless samurai's chest.

An interesting device the ninja used was called a shuko. This implement, which was worn on the hands like a glove, would allow him to grip relatively smooth, hard surfaces. It was primarily an instrument for climbing, for example to scale castle walls to gain entry into a lord's private quarters for a possible assassination. This weapon could also be used for trapping and holding the blade of an attacker's sword, while the ninja pulled another weapon out of his tunic to finish him off. The implement was made of one narrow and one wide metal band joined by a flat metal section. The narrow band slipped over the hand and tightened around the wrist, leaving the wide band to encircle the hand. Underneath, on the palm side of the wide band, protruded four sharp spikes. The spikes were often raked across an enemy's face in close combat, and the back of the metal band could be used to break the attacker's jaw.

Perhaps the most famous weapon of the ninja was the shuriken, the star-shaped missile that was thrown with deadly accuracy. Although multi-pointed shuriken were the ones most commonly used, many other shapes were included, such as a

many of the martial arts. If he were suddenly confronted by a sword-wielding samurai, the ninja with a jerk of the wrist could flick the end off the bamboo pole to reveal a six-foot-long chain. This could be hurled at the oncoming aggressor to wrap around his sword arm, to ensnare him, or aimed at his legs to jerk him off balance

triangle, swastika, or flat oval resembling the blade of a knife. Most ninja carried nine shuriken, hidden in a pocket of the tunic, but within easy reach if they were needed in an emergency. Nine was considered a lucky number. Throughout his childhood years the young ninja would practise throwing the shuriken into trees and at other targets, until his aim, accuracy and timing became second nature. These weapons were usually held between the thumb and forefinger, and hurled, perhaps, at some unsuspecting castle guard out alone on sentry duty. Maximum effective range of the shuriken was limited to about 30 feet (9m).

The ninja often used shuriken as a distraction, to make good his escape. He would hurl six or seven of them from his open palm, so fast, that all six would be in the air at the same time before the first one struck home. The razor-sharp stars whizzing through the air would throw an assailant into total confusion. It was well known that the ninja tipped the points with a deadly poison and that even the slightest scratch would mean instant death. Because shuriken were black they could be thrown virtually invisibly into a dark room. Faced with certain death hurling through the air and not knowing which way it was coming, even the hardened samurai would no doubt be terror-stricken. A ninja would always retain at least one shuriken upon his person for close-quarter combat. An enemy struggling with a cornered ninja could suddenly find a very sharp shuriken placed under his armpit and his arm forced downwards on to the evil points.

It would be impossible to name every weapon that a ninja used in his arsenal, for the simple fact that he utilized anything that came to hand. The ninja's ingenuity knew no bounds. Sometimes he would prepare special weapons to use solely for one particular mission. These ranged from hollowed-out egg shells filled with explosives, to create havoc or merely act as a diversion to allow him access, or arrows fitted with ingenious devices that would explode on contact, to incendiary arrows, or poison-tipped arrows. All could be used to give the ninja the necessary extra time to ply his deadly trade.

The art of camouflage

The art of hiding and camouflage, known as inpo, was the speciality of the ninja warrior. He took advantage of every possible object, natural as well as man-made, to conceal himself from the enemy. This ability helped to give rise to the legends that

NINJUTSU

1 Concealed in a bush, the ninja is barely detectable. He prepares to attack with a kusari-gama, an ensnaring weapon.

2 The chain is released and moves in a circular motion.

3 It ensnares the opponent's sword.

ninja could make themselves invisible at will. The trained ninja could blend in with his surroundings in any situation, no matter where he was. If being pursued in the countryside, he would dash behind a rock or fallen stump or climb high into the branches of a tree. Because of the in-depth training methods given to him in his youth, he was able to concentrate his mind, shape his hands into the mystical finger-knitting pattern that applied to his particular situation and totally melt into his surroundings. Once in the correct frame of mind, the ninja could shape his body to correspond with his environment. He could curl up into a ball and look just like another stone or boulder, which would prove very con-fusing to his pursuers looking for a man with arms and legs. If chased through a dense forest the ninja could assume the pose of a tree. He could wrap himself around a branch to become part of the tree. Since he was a master at controlled breathing techniques, he was able to remain motionless for long periods of time. Ninja would often bury themselves in the ground completely, except for a thin bamboo snorkel to breathe through.

Such camouflage could assist in creating the perfect ambush. When the particular target came along, a lord returning to his castle or out on a hunting trip perhaps the ninja would suddenly strike, then vanish into his surroundings to wait for the fuss to die down before making good his escape. Those retainers left behind would wonder what mysterious hand of wrath had struck their lord down.

The female ninja

Female ninja, known as kunoichi, were an important part of their clans. They too, like their male counterparts, were trained in the warrior ways of ninjutsu. But when they reached puberty, a more distinctive training regimen was implemented. With their female allure coming more to the fore, the kunoichi were trained in the delicate ways of the geisha, but their ultimate intentions were far more sinister.

It has been said that a single well-placed kunoichi could wreak more damage in certain situations then her male counter-

4 The ninja can now attack with the blade end of his weapon. He also sweeps away the swordsman's supporting leg.

5 The swordsman goes crashing to the ground. He is now at the mercy of the ninja.

111

UNARMED NINJUTSU

1 *As an assailant moves in with a punch, the ninja, instead of blocking, counters with a blow to the soft inner arm, causing instant pain.*

2 *Using his thumb knuckle as the weapon, the ninja aims at the throat of the attacker. Meanwhile his right hand acts as a defence.*

3 *The thumb strikes goes in and the attacker jerks his head backwards. But the ninja is ready with a palm grab to the head. He keeps an arched body to prevent a groin attack.*

part. One of her main functions was to gather intelligence. Methods of seduction were taught to her so that she could use sex as a weapon. She could always gain entry to a household or castle by passing herself off as a serving maid or prostitute. The unsuspecting samurai guards would hardly notice her as she came and went each day. But all the time the kunoichi was looking, learning and assimilating everything that might be of use to the ninja agent to gain entry at a later date. She might collect information on the build-up of troops and weapons at a particular place and pass this on to a rival lord. He would have paid handsomely for such knowledge.

In the middle of the sixteenth century, Japan saw one of the most infamous kunoichi warriors actually form her own school. Her name was Chiyome Mochizu-ki. She trained a group of shrine attendants, called miko, to act as spies for her uncle. These young girls travelled around the area attending to their religious duties. Without arousing attention they would gather intelligence of strength of forces and hidden fortifications and pass it on.

A woman could often move unsuspected in circles where a male agent would find it impossible to blend in. The weapons she carried were just as awesome as the male ninja's but not as detectable. Kunoichi specialized in poisons and drugs, small knives and needles, hairpins and combs.

With these tools she could always protect herself and yet at the same time get close to a lord. While he was lost in her charms she would implement whatever instructions she had been given.

The modern ninja
Recently, the popularity of the martial arts has included a tremendous interest in the art of ninjutsu. A current ninja boom is being enjoyed in the United States. Today's practitioners, however, are not bent upon death and destruction. They are often already competent in one or other sphere of the martial arts. Their sole aim is to gain a greater understanding of the martial systems through the study of ninjutsu, an art that has often been termed 'the complete way of living'. Ninjutsu encompasses more than just combat methods; it enters into the realms of parapsychology. Its practitioners deem the art to be a pattern for living.

By its very nature, with secrecy its foremost principle, it is difficult to know if any of the ninja clans are actually still in existence, though instructors are not hard to find. In Japan the greatest living authority on the art of ninjutsu is Dr Masaaki Hatsumi who is the present grandmaster of the Togakure ryu ninjutsu. He is a direct descendant of the Iga line and its 34th headmaster. Dr Hatsumi believes that personal enlightenment can only come about through total immersion in the martial

4 While pivoting to the side the ninja smashes the attacker's head into his shoulder.

5 The ninja drops his hand quickly to guard against a possible counter and then forces his knee into the attacker's leg so that he loses balance. A smart blow to the calf from his knee will cause considerable pain.

tradition as a complete way of living.

Unarmed fighting

Tai-jutsu is the ninja method of fighting without weapons. But unlike other empty-handed Japanese systems, tai-jutsu stresses the body dynamics, the principle of using the whole of the body as a weapon. Fighting stance is always determined by the relationship of the fighter to his opponent; there is no basic stance.

Although this may appear to be something of a contradiction, there are actually four main fighting positions, but these are only used as a framework for the student, so that he can gain understanding of how tai-jutsu operates. These four fighting positions consist of the natural stance, defensive stance, offensive stance and receiving stance. This latter stance seems, at first glance, to have similarities with the aikido principle. It makes use of evasion and then countering. It is sometimes interpreted as inviting an attack, or misinterpreted as surrendering to one. This is because the practitioner stands there in a relaxed manner with his arms and legs spread wide open, as though he were about to give in. As the attack commences, the tai-jutsu exponent appears to vanish, but then suddenly rises up behind the attacker, to mete out justice of his own.

Because tai-jutsu is strictly a combat martial art, the aim of its proponents is to inflict the greatest possible damage with the fewest moves and easiest methods. The art encompasses grappling, throws and escapes, locks, chokes, and muscle and bone attacks. All the time the student has to control the fight; once the control is lost, so is the fight itself.

The key to this efficient and effective movement is coordinated rhythm. For obvious reasons, any encounter is a spontaneous and sudden action, that requires a response without even thinking. To enable the ninja student to train for this, certain special exercises were devised to act as a foundation. These roughly break down into four training methods: sparring, target hitting, shadow boxing and visualization. The first three sections are self-explanatory. The fourth—visualization—is employed to increase the student's awareness, and to use this awareness to assimilate the principles of various body movements. The aim is actually to visualize in the training hall the effects of certain attacks and counters, under controlled conditions, thereby training the consciousness to develop a kind of sixth sense. The concept is that if you can read a situation before it happens, then you can never be surprised by an attack.

The art of ninjutsu grew up as an outlawed counter-culture to that of the accepted samurai society. Yet today its philosophies and fighting methods live on.

113

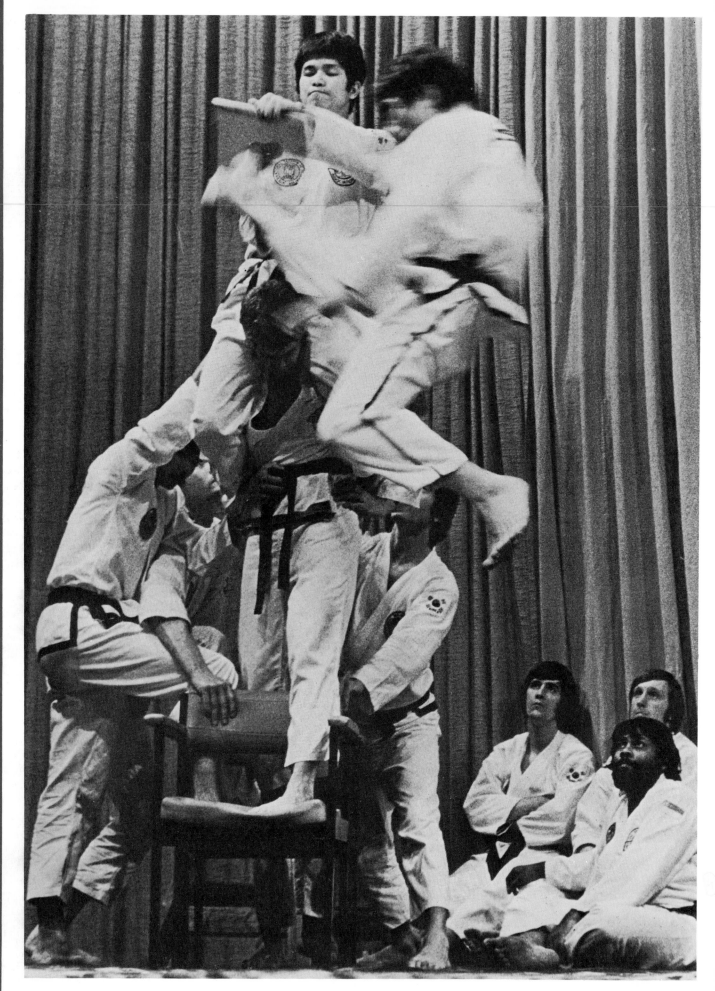

THE MARTIAL ARTS OF KOREA

'A man who has attained mastery of an art reveals it in his every action.'

It could be said that today, in the twentieth century, the Korean martial arts have finally reached full maturity. After centuries of suppression, not least in the first half of this present one, ancient indigenous methods of unarmed combat have finally emerged and, in the form of modern taekwon-do, are now practised in over 80 countries with simply millions of students.

Taekwon-do

The name, literally translated, means 'way of the foot and fist'. Although a modern concept, its roots can be traced back some 1,400 years to a tiny kingdom at the southern tip of the Korean peninsula, called Silla. This kingdom was under constant attack from its two neighbours, Baek Je to the west and Koguryo to the north. It was essential that Silla should build a powerful fighting force with strong leadership in order to maintain its independence, and with this aim in view, the young aristocrats under the 24th king, Chin Heung, formed themselves into an élite warrior class named the Hwa-rangdo or 'way of the flowering manhood'. They practised strict mental and physical discipline and followed a code of conduct set out by the wise Korean Buddhist monk and scholar, Won Kang:

1 Be loyal to your king.
2 Be obedient to your parents.
3 Be honourable to your friends.
4 Never retreat in battle.
5 Make a just kill.

These young warriors practised the traditional weapon arts using the spear, bow, sword and hook. It is also well established that they incorporated local forms of unarmed hand and foot fighting into their repertoire, mainly taek kyon and soo-bak. By adding a mental concept to soo-bak, it eventually became a true art form with the name of soo-bak-gi.

There is a stone carving in a cave of a famous warrior of the period, Kumkang-Yuksa, showing a clenched fist, a distinct knife hand and muscled legs—obviously the result of hard physical training. Indeed, the Hwa-rangdo's regimen included climbing precipitous mountains and swimming in freezing rivers to toughen themselves up. These warriors became famous for their courage, gaining respect even from their enemies, so outstanding was their skill in battle.

Silla's victories under the leadership of the Hwa-rangdo, together with an alliance with China, eventually united the three kingdoms for a while.

In Koguryo to the north, the most popular method of unarmed fighting was soo bak-gi. A mural in a tomb painted during the age of the 10th king of Koguryo, clearly shows flying kicks, recognizable in modern taekwon-do. Competitions in soo bak were held twice a year, along with wrestling, tug-of-war and other sports.

In AD 953 the kingdom of Silla was overthrown and the Koryo dynasty was established. All martial arts were still actively encouraged because the peninsula's survival rested on maintaining a strong army. One king held an annual contest of unarmed combat on Ma Am mountain. This was compulsory for all the soldiers, but the prize was enticing—a prestigious government appointment. Twenty-five postures had to be mastered by practitioners, including hand and leg techniques together with falling, rolling, jumping and pulling. The fact that three winners subsequently became important generals no doubt proves the effectiveness of the training. During the Silla and Koryo dynasties, it would be true to say that the Korean martial arts reached a peak of perfection.

Somewhat later, in the early fifteenth century, the third king of the Yi dynasty was also actively supporting the martial arts

Left A high-flying front kick such as this can break a board held up to ten feet (3m) from the ground. The striking area is the ball of the foot.

115

by recruiting experts in taek kyon, sirum (Korean wrestling), archery and soo bak-gi into his army. But an era of peace followed, resulting in strong anti-military feelings, and the Hwa-rang were disbanded. By the end of the dynasty the martial arts had virtually died out and were practised only in secret, mainly in Buddhist temples.

In recent times the martial arts were once again forbidden in Korea; this was during the Japanese occupation of the country from 1909-1945, when it was in the invaders' interest to suppress the Korean nationalist spirit. Despite this, taek kyon was secretly kept alive.

General Choi Hong Hi

Choi was born in a harsh rugged area of what is now North Korea. When young, he was frail and unwell, but showed his determined nationalist spirit even as a child. When he was twelve he was expelled from school because he was agitating against Japanese authorities.

Choi's father sent him to learn calligraphy from the master Han Il Dong, who also taught him taek kyon. This made him much stronger. Subsequently imprisoned by the Japanese because of further nationalist involvement, Choi used his time to develop these martial skills. Both his cell-mate and even his gaoler were soon his pupils. Later he also gained a black belt in karate.

When Choi returned to Korea he joined the Pyongyang student soldier's movement. He was in charge of security. He was then captured by the Japanese police and sentenced to death. When World War II was over he was luckily released.

After the liberation, Choi joined the new Korean army and rose rapidly to the highest rank. He taught his martial skills to his men to make them better soldiers. Realizing that they needed a truly Korean art, he dedicated himself to developing his own style to the very highest level, calling it Chang Hun. It is based on taek kyon, soo bak-gi and karate, together with many new techniques scientifically devised and refined by himself. It was his suggestion that this Korean martial art should be given the name of taekwon-do, having a close similarity to the ancient name of taek kyon, and on 11 April 1955 at a special conference this name was accepted. The next year the first competitive championships were held and shortly afterwards taekwon-do gained government recognition in Korea as a national sport. In 1988 it will be a demonstration item at the olympics in Seoul.

Today, not only is taekwon-do a means of promoting the Korean culture around the world, but it also offers a sophisticated method of self-protection.

Taekwon-do training

The practitioner is informed that taekwon-do's activities are defensive rather than offensive in spirit, an attitude that parallels Korea's own character as a nation. The art teaches not only effective self-defence, but beauty of form, in addition to a striving towards positive moral rearmament. There are five tenets set out by General Choi which must be upheld and these are courtesy, integrity, perseverance, self-control and indomitable spirit.

The place of training is termed a do jang. The practice suit (dobok) comprises white cotton trousers and wrap-over jacket edged in black. This is completed by a coloured belt denoting rank. There are ten preliminary grades (gups) before first dan black belt, starting with white belt and graduating through yellow, green, blue and red. These colours carry with them particular meanings: white signifies innocence, yel-

Below Master Rhee Ki Ha, *who first took taekwon-do to the UK, performs the famous split kick with apparent ease. The inscription above the picture reads: 'To the best student ever of taekwon-do from the founder.'*

low the earth in which a plant takes root, green the plant's growth, blue the heaven towards which it matures, and red signifies danger, warning the student to exercise caution. Black symbolizes imperviousness to darkness and fear, but even with first dan the student is still considered a novice. Only at fourth dan does he or she enter the expert class and at seventh joins the exclusive élite of masters. Throughout, students are not just graded for physical skills, but for character development, fortitude and tenacity.

Training usually begins with students practising in lines, starting with basic exercises and techniques. Patterns must also be learnt so that complete fluency is attained in all the movements. They must gradually become familiar with the 69 vital spots (kup so) of the body, which are classified into major and minor: blows to the former can cause fatalities or permanent deformity, and to the latter severe pain and malfunctioning of organs. Knowledge must also be gained of the best mode of attack for each spot. But theory is not enough and all such information must be rehearsed in the form of sparring, cautiously at first with pre-arranged methods of attack and defence using three, two or one steps. In this it is decided beforehand what the target is to be and which tool is to be employed. The counter-attack is limited to one move only. One-step sparring is considered to be of prime importance, since it epitomizes taekwon-do's aim of victory with a single blow. A completely accurate, speedy and decisive blow must be delivered to a vital spot with the correct weapon. After this, the student can move on to semi-free sparring in which one attack and defence are exchanged, both techniques being open to choice. Then he or she is finally ready for free sparring.

Perhaps the most typically Korean part of the syllabus is foot sparring, directly developed from taek kyon, in which no hand techniques are allowed. These include such manoeuvres as a side piercing kick, reverse turning kick, hooking kick, as well as a number of spectacular mid-air kicks, both linear and turning. Indeed, exponents of taekwon-do are famous for their devas-

Right At a demonstration, 8th dan Master Rhee performs the incredibly difficult flying twin-foot kick, breaking blocks of wood with both feet simultaneously.

117

SPARRING

PATTERNS

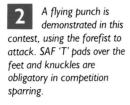

1 Many women take up taekwon-do for fitness and self-defence. Here a lady practitioner just completes a flying reverse turning kick in which the heel of the foot is used as the striking area.

2 A flying punch is demonstrated in this contest, using the forefist to attack. SAF 'T' pads over the feet and knuckles are obligatory in competition sparring.

There are 24 patterns to be learnt in taekwon-do. This one is known as Hwa-rang. The North Korean team perform it here in perfect synchronization.

tating kicks and justly so. They can launch themselves off the ground gaining heights of up to ten feet (3m) and deliver a whole series of kicks while still in mid-air. But the beginner has a long way to go before acquiring such awe-inspiring expertise.

Patterns of movement

In taekwon-do these are known as tul. Practice of tul allows the usage of potentially dangerous techniques in perfect safety, as the person executing the pattern fights only an imaginary opponent. Just like a karate kata, taekwon-do's tul acts as an aid to binding the basic techniques together in a coordinated and fluid motion. When the

beginner advances on to the more ambitious techniques of taekwon-do, there is a tul or pattern available. There are 24 patterns of varying degrees of difficulty, leading ultimately to complete mastery of a wide variety of techniques. The number 24 is taken from the hours in the day. General Choi feels that each person's life is but a day in terms of the universe. He therefore offers the 24 patterns to all students of taekwon-do, just as he has dedicated his whole life to the art.

Repetition is the key for gaining maximum potential from the patterns. Constant practice with the same pattern day after day eventually produces an almost

118

automatic performance. This ability to integrate complicated techniques, without having to think about them, creates a state of mind in which the practitioner can react to danger instinctively, and reply to an attack with a counter or block without bringing into play his conscious thought. This way valuable 'reaction time' is saved.

In taekwon-do, the first pattern that is learned is called Chon-ji. Chon-ji means the origin of all things in the universe. It consists of two similar parts—one to represent heaven and the other the earth. This is a simple pattern and has only 19 movements. The rudiments of how the first basic techniques are knitted together are ably portrayed in this first form.

Many of the patterns have been given names of illustrious Korean people. The idea is to take on something of the character of that person when performing a particular pattern, whether it be nobility, courage, wisdom or military discipline.

Stretching and training aids

Superb power kicks for combat do not just come naturally through basic training. They have to be worked at with a series of physically demanding stretching exercises. Taekwon-do-ists aim for flexibility in the legs, because this is essential for speed, which in turn provides the power upon impact.

In any stretching programme certain rules have to be observed to ensure complete safety. For instance, muscles should always be given a chance to stretch of their own accord. In exercising, one should never push, jolt, bounce or move sharply, thus putting undue tension on the delicate muscle structures. Everything is done smoothly without force. Stretching should never be practised before warming up with other preliminary exercises.

For advanced students, a puller is recommended to assist with the stretching of the legs. This is constructed from a strong rope which is passed through two pulleys fixed to the ceiling four feet (1.2m) apart. The student loops one end around one foot and holds the other end in his or her hand. By pulling, the kicking leg can be supported on the rope, increasing height and perfecting the various angles of attack.

Bags are also considered to be helpful training aids. A large one is used for the practice of full-impact kicks and punches and provides a safe way of learning complicated flying foot techniques. A round or long ball fastened between the ceiling and floor with rubber or elastic thongs provides a flexible target; this develops good timing and speed in both punches and kicks. A post, similar to karate's makiwara, is also employed to increase the effectiveness of punches.

Power and destruction

General Choi has spent his entire life in analysing and refining taekwon-do. One result of this dedicated work has been a 15-volume encyclopedia, the first of its kind, which catalogues 3,200 techniques. Particularly noticeable is his application of scientific principles to produce the most effective results. His theory of power (him ui wolli) is a fascinating study on its own.

To gain a high degree of physical power it is necessary to give individual attention to the following: reaction force, concentration, equilibrium, breath control and speed. If practice is devoted to each of these, then students will eventually realize

DESTRUCTION

1 A reverse knife-hand strike is the technique chosen to break these pieces of pine. Here the demonstrator, a UK team member, measures up.

2 Despite the fact that the pieces of wood are each one inch (2.5cm) thick, he breaks them all with a single blow.

SPECIAL TECHNIQUES

After gaining a black belt, the taekwon-do practitioner is allowed to attempt the special techniques, which normally involve flying over large obstacles before applying some kind of destruction while still in mid-air.

1 *In this case several men and a motorcycle are the obstacles and a piece of wood has to be broken.*

2 *The demonstrator leaps into the air in a flying side piercing kick.*

3 *He breaks the wood with the outer edge of his foot before landing.*

Right *Another popular obstacle is a pyramid of men. It takes many years of training to reach this level of ability.*

their true potential in terms of power.

Reaction force consists of two forces combined: the opponent's force rushing forwards, and the reaction force produced from within the defender, for example by pulling the left fist back to the hip as the right fist counters with a punch.

Concentration implies the application of impact force on to the smallest target area. Everyone knows how easily a stiletto heel can dent even the hardest floors. Careful selection of a vital spot is also essential.

No blow can be effective unless the body is well balanced. Students must therefore learn correct stance, with the centre of gravity running on a straight line midway between both legs if the weight is distributed equally between them, or in the centre of the foot if the weight is on that foot. For this reason, the heel of the supporting leg must be kept on the ground when kicking.

A sharp exhalation of breath at the moment of impact helps to focus the attack. The resulting tensing of abdominal muscles also increases power and at the same time can help condition the body to withstand blows without injury.

Speed is perhaps the most important factor of all. Mathematically, force equals mass times acceleration. Mass, or body weight, can be added from the hip, or from the springing action of the knee joint. In a series of experiments conducted by General Choi it was discovered that well-executed taekwon-do punches and kicks were faster than normal reflex time. They are therefore impossible to block unless detected beforehand. For this reason, students are trained to look always at the opponent's eyes and never at the arms or legs.

The best way to test power is without doubt in the destruction of objects such as roofing tiles or pieces of wood, and taekwon-do lays particular stress on destruction techniques in its training syllabus. Women as well as men are encouraged to test their own skills in this way, but children are excluded in case of damage to growing tissue. Application of the scientific principles outlined above together with correct training in taekwon-do techniques can produce the most astonishing results, even from a slightly built woman. Moreover, successful breaks help to build the self-confidence of the students and make them aware of the awesome power which lies within themselves.

The state of the art

In 1961 all the old groups of Korean martial arts united under the banner of the Korean Taekwon-do Association, with General Choi elected as the first president. To spread the art around the world, the general founded the ITF on 22 March 1966 with nine countries: Korea, USA, West Germany, Italy, Singapore, Turkey, Malaysia, Vietnam and the United Arab Republic. As its first ambassador he gave many demonstrations. One of his main aims has always been to promote peace between all nations through his art of taekwon-do. To further this ideal he finally decided to settle in Canada and took the ITF with him. Meanwhile a new president for the KTA was elected named Yung Chai Kin. In 1973 he created another governing body called the World Taekwon-do Federation. This new body quickly set about developing a distinction between their taekwon-do and the general's style.

Today, these two international organizations are responsible for the practice of about 80 per cent of all taekwon-do.

WTF competitions are fought with contestants wearing body armour. This consists of a padded breast-plate fastening at the rear, hand mitts or gloves, also padded, and a special instep guard made from a foam-like polystyrene. This 'shoe' fits over the foot but has no sole. Full-contact kicks

Above *Another special technique is this flying long side kick over two hurdles. The photograph gives an idea of the distance which has to be covered. Moreover, the exponent must break a block of wood before landing. To add to his difficulties the wood in this case is held in only one hand, so unless he exerts sufficient speed on impact, the timber will simply fly away and not break.*

Left *General Choi Hong Hi, founder of taekwon-do and President of the ITF (International Taekwon-do Federation), is seen on the left of this picture. He holds the highest degree of black belt – 9th dan. Behind him is Master Rhee Ki Ha, OCM Korea, 8th dan master instructor. He founded the UKTA (UK Taekwon-do Association) in 1967, the RITA (Republic of Ireland Taekwon-do Association) in 1968 and the AETF (All European Taekwon-do Federation) in 1979. He is Vice-President of the ITF.*

and punches are delivered to specific target areas on the body and depending on the part struck, the contestant is awarded a certain number of points. By contrast, ITF contestants wear what is called SAF'T' on the hands and feet, developed in the late 1970s by 8th dan Master Rhee Jhoon to prevent accidents and protect the opponent from contact. In this style punches and kicks must stop fractionally short of the target.

Korea is a country that has seen much strife over the past 50 years. Its martial arts have been suppressed and then subjected to political interference. But the spirit of taekwon-do has emerged, carrying forward the martial heritage of 1,400 years.

Hapkido

Hapkido is another Korean martial art, but distinctively different from taekwon-do. The word means 'way of coordinated power'. The art exists almost exclusively for self-defence purposes. In hapkido there are no formalized patterns or sporting links.

The art is unusual for the fact that it emphasizes a non-violent code of counter-defence. In an attack situation, the hapkido practitioner will remain calm until the aggressor has made the initial advance and committed himself to a strike situation. The hapkido-ist then simply applies a soft circular block to deflect the approaching blow. This is followed by an explosion of counter-offensive techniques, that can result in the attacker being annihilated.

Hapkido combines the same principles found in aikido with the strong kicks and punches from Korea's indigenous taek kyon. Some kicks are almost acrobatic in their delivery, with mid-air strikes using both feet at the same time. The art is composed of three primary skills: non-resistance when meeting force, circular motions in countering and attacking, and the 'water principle'.

When the hapkido practitioner counters, he or she does it with ultimate strength and total intent of purpose. It is for these reasons that hapkido-ists do not indulge in sporting competition. The art also incorporates blows to the vital areas, as well as locks and leverage holds.

Hapkido-ists believe that knocking an attacker to the ground is not enough because he might get back up and attack again. The hapkido practitioner must judge whether the assailant is a threat to his or her own life, and if so, must finish him off. This attitude is very different from that of

Left *The World Taekwon-do Federation encourages competition sparring and allows contact blows to the body. Here a Korean exponent aims a high kick at his opponent.*

the aikido-ist, who has to be content to leave an attacker helpless but unhurt.

The water principle

When water runs down a hillside, instead of crashing into obstacles it always goes around them. This is imitated in the hapkido art by never meeting an attack with a solid block. Instead, the practitioner steps to the outside of the attack and deflects the blow, taking the force of that attack around his or her body, thus accepting the movement and neutralizing it in a circular motion. The point is not to resist an opponent, but to go with the attack, ride it, and then take advantage of the opponent's own movement.

Because hapkido has not been diluted by sporting considerations, many of its techniques have remained unadulterated and consequently 100 per cent effective. Strength is not essential in hapkido, and therefore many women have adopted the art as a practical means of self-defence.

One of the most important aspects of hapkido training is the avoidance of pre-set forms of sparring. Hapkido impresses upon the practitioner the necessity of continuously flowing attacks. Counters must be fast, flowing and rhythmical, until the assailant is completely stopped.

Hapkido history

Chronologically, the history of hapkido does not reach very far back in time, although it does have links with Korea's Buldo mu sool (Buddhist monks' martial arts). Its modern resurrection was due to a man named Yong Shul Choi. In 1910 Choi went to Japan and studied a martial art that was a blend of the old Japanese aiki-jutsu and jiu-jitsu, called Daito ryu aiki-jitsu, under Shokaku Takeda. Choi did not return to his homeland for almost 40 years. Upon his return after World War II, Choi introduced his hapkido to Korea. At first it was received with little enthusiasm as the art proved very difficult to master. Also, at about the same time taekwon-do was beginning to unify. However a select group of stalwarts pursued their endeavours and eventually mastered hapkido, thus helping to perpetuate this dynamic art.

Hapkido's development on a world scale is largely due to a Korean master named Bong Soo Han. It was he who introduced the art to the US special service groups in his capacity as an unarmed combat instructor in Vietnam. He later went to live in America himself. Being a direct student of Choi, Han was allowed to open his own academy of hapkido.

The sulsa of Korea

The sulsa were a warrior élite who can find their equivalents among the Japanese ninja. This secret sect, who stemmed from the hwarang-do, were masters of espionage and silent killing techniques. Their training was so extreme that other warriors often classed them as a type of one-man army. Students eligible to learn this art were picked from the cream of the Hwa-rangdo ranks. A modern parallel is the selection from special groups such as the Royal Marine Commandos in Britain, of entrants to the exclusive SAS.

The sulsa's training guided him through martial art skills that could be geared to meet every encounter. They could walk on water using special boat-like shoes, scale sheer castle walls with ease and, with carefully adapted kites, they were able to soar over enemy positions taking count of their fortifictations. Unlike the ninja, the sulsa were not picked and trained from birth.

The sulsa today

The principles of sulsa training have been adapted by many of the world's armed services, most notably the US Rangers, who were taught these skills by the late Mike Echanis. Echanis had been a student of hwarang-do under the grandmaster Joo Bang Lee. Lee taught him much of this ancient knowledge and Echanis expanded it with some of his own ideas. Modern psychology became involved, and Echanis trained service personnel in thought-control and meditation.

Since then, the martial arts of the sulsa have been taught to non-military people and interest in this fighting method is growing among modern martial arts enthusiasts.

Tang soo do

Like so many of the present-day Korean martial arts, Tang soo do is relatively new with roots reaching back into Korea's ancient fighting past. Its original name was soo bahk do, but it was changed by its modern founder Master Hwang Kee. In Korea, however, it is still known by its former name.

In 1945 Hwang Kee founded the Moo Duk Kwan, loosely translated as 'Institute of Martial Virtue', to promote the study of Tang soo do. Great confusion exists between Moo Duk Kwan and Tang soo do. The former is the organization and headquarters in Seoul, whereas the latter is the actual name of the art. Master Kee did not create Tang soo do; he only renamed it. It means 'way of the T'ang dynasty hand'.

Master Hwang Kee was born in an area of Korea now known as the Demilitarized Zone. In his early twenties he travelled to China to study their martial arts. During his nine years there, Hwang Kee was exposed to many different styles and systems. As well as martial arts training, he was also an avid student of Chinese philosophy and classical writings. At the end of World War II he returned home and founded his own establishment.

Tang soo do is thought of as a way of life by its practitioners, rather than a means of self-defence, with the belief that the spiritual life must be balanced with the physical life to create a harmony. Tang soo do places much emphasis upon kicking techniques, rather than on hand manoeuvres. Its ultimate tenet is self-improvement through the art. Tournaments and competitions are held on a regular basis, with strict rules as regards behaviour and the proper etiquette of fighting.

Students begin in the art by learning the five basic hyungs (patterns). Interestingly, these forms bear a remarkable resemblance to the Japanese Heian katas. There are some people who think that Tang soo do, in part at least, is really a disguised form of Japanese Shotokan karate, with the addition of the indigenous Korean high kicks.

THE WORLD OF MARTIAL ARTS

'Ten thousand rivers flow into the sea; the sea is never full.'

Finally we come to various martial arts which are less well known in the West. However, their development in different parts of the world adds to the rich variety of arts that will always continue to fascinate the true devotee.

Thai boxing

One of the most devastating arts ever to come out of Asia is that of muay Thai or Thai boxing. This lethal martial art is dedicated to pure fighting and is without forms or kata. The training is hard, gruelling and intensive, usually beginning at around ten years old and exponents are noted for their courage and fighting spirit, plus total commitment to their art.

When instruction commences in muay Thai, the first thing that is taught is footwork and leg movement. Co-ordination is vital, because the pattern of the footwork dictates the range of the fighter's attack and defence. Both legs work together all the time, unlike many styles of karate and kung fu in which one leg can remain motionless for some of the time. The Thai boxer justifies the constant motion by commenting that a moving target is always harder to hit than a static one. The new student then learns the punching techniques: how to execute a correct jab, uppercut, straight punch and cross punch. These are then brought into synchronization with the legs and footwork.

In Thai boxing there are no basics as such. When the student can perform two or three punching techniques reasonably well, he or she will be taught how to combine them into an attack. The groundwork of introductory techniques is covered fairly quickly.

At first sight muay Thai training may seem a little similar to that of Western boxing, but any similarity quickly ceases with the introduction into training of the Thai fighter's secret weapon: the yng kow

or long knee. This constitutes a defence and an attack all in one. Particular attention must be paid to balance and body posture. The long knee can be used to attack the stomach or sternum area. It can be converted from a short-range into a long-range weapon merely by extending the leg and suddenly it becomes a strong front thrust kick. The fighter learns to raise the knee when attacked so that it becomes an effective shield to guard the groin and lower body area. With the hand held in a high guard, the Thai fighter uses the same leg to retaliate.

Because Thai boxing is based upon close-range fighting, beginners have to learn the knee and elbow techniques first. The Thai fighter gradually moves on to mid-range movements which teach him to execute many of the lethal kicks. Unlike many other martial artists, a Thai boxer trains to kick with the shin rather than the ball, or instep, of the foot. This application of the shin makes the roundhouse kick deadly. The shin is regarded as the Thai fighter's major weapon of attack and destruction. Traditionally, the popular method for hardening the shin was the repeated kicking of a banana tree. Today, this training has transferred to a sand-filled leather bag.

Thai boxing leads the way with stamina training. A combat might continue over a long period, so the fighter must have the energy to maintain the attack and defence effectively for as long as possible. A daily training regimen can involve a long jog for as far as five miles or so. Swimming is also stressed. The fighters go straight into daily training as soon as they have finished their jog. This arduous regimen is repeated day after day. Upon first sight the muay Thai fighter appears rather lean, resembling a half-starved waif. This is probably the greatest misconception ever to arise about a martial artist.

The whole of muay Thai training is geared towards effectiveness in combat.

Left The ladies' World Champion in Thai boxing, Lisa Howarth, scores a winning point against her opponent. Women in this sport demonstrate just the same aggressive fighting spirit as men and risk similar blows to the body.

Even the simple warming-up exercises that are practised have a purposeful application. Nothing is wasted. For instance, one exercise that stretches the leg and also makes the torso supple is the knee-to-shoulder lift. This involves raising the right knee to the right shoulder and the left to the left shoulder. Apart from the benefits previously mentioned, this is the actual technique employed to guard against kicks to the body.

The target areas for strikes and kicks are termed pont or point. Therefore high point, middle point and low point refer to head, chest and below the belt respectively. It is to the low-point area that the Thai boxer concentrates most attacking techniques. This is a point above the knee and below the waist round about the upper thigh area. A series of blows to this centre can, at worst, actually knock a man out. Failing that, it incapacitates the opponent to such an extent that his legs go and he crumbles to the floor beaten. Beginners in the art improve their focus by hitting and kicking special leather bags held by a partner.

Any framework is only as strong as its support. The idea in the mind of the Thai boxer is to attack that framework from the bottom and the rest will come tumbling down.

Muay Thai history

The early records of Siam, as Thailand was once known, show that the unarmed art of Thai boxing has been practised since ancient times. There is evidence that it formed part of a military training syllabus. Throughout its 2,000 years of history, this royal land has resisted all attempts to conquer her, which probably gives a lot of credit to the fighting spirit of the people. Siam, in her geographical position of South East Asia, is bordered by Burma, Laos, Cambodia and Malaysia. With warring tribes constantly biting at her heels Siam had to maintain a tremendous will to survive.

It is known that early muay Thai was influenced to a large extent by various Chinese boxing methods, but because the Thai people were combative by nature, they developed a system that was geared to be effective yet quickly learned. This might explain why many of the muay Thai special fighting techniques are not seen anywhere else outside Thailand. It is thought that the wandering Buddhist priests first introduced unarmed fighting methods and that the Thai people then developed them indepen-

dently. Old Siam was a staunchly Buddhist culture, as is modern Thailand. It had a monarchy whose every dictate was followed without question by the people. When it was suggested that the commonfolk should learn the unarmed combat arts of the military, they complied instantly. Consequently, even the simple farmers high in the mountains gained rudimentary skills in muay Thai.

Gradually the old Chinese boxing methods became altered beyond recognition, and the skills took on a true Siamese character. Over a period of years, when the armies of the king had vanquished all would-be invaders, an era of peace prevailed. The skills of the unarmed fighters were maintained by the village communities, who turned the art into a sport. A great king named Pra Chao Sua, often known as the 'tiger king', was so proficient in muay Thai that he would often leave his palace disguised as a peasant, just so that he could take part in village boxing events and test his skills against the local champions. He was so involved in every aspect of the art that he would leave his courtly duties in the hands of his brother and go out into the courtyard and train for up to six hours a day with his soldiers. Interestingly, King Pra Chao Sua developed many new techni-

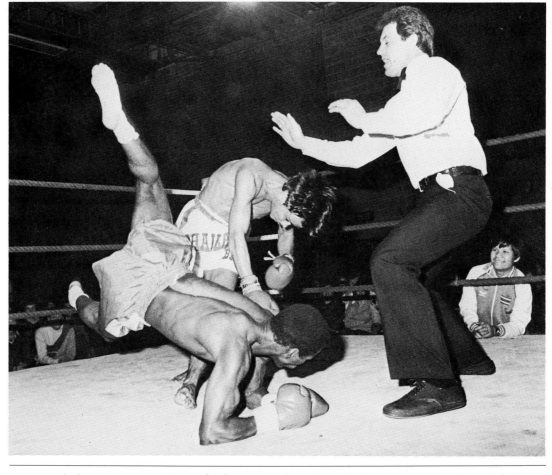

ques and boxing strategies which were adopted into training systems; today they are still used under the name of the 'tiger king style'.

Many stories emanate from Thai boxing circles about their legendary heroes, but the one name that stands out above all others is the fourteenth-century hero Nai Khanom Dtom. This hero was captured during a battle with Thailand's Burmese enemies. The King of Burma had heard many tales of Nai Khanom Dtom's prowess as a bare-handed fighter, so he put him to a test whereby, if he was successful, he could earn his freedom. All Nai had to do was defeat Burma's twelve greatest warriors in the gladiatorial arena. The fight was to be to the death. From early morning until dusk, the proud Thai warrior defeated all who came against him. Many of the Burmese spectators who had been cheering for their own men suddenly switched allegiance in honour of their enemy's valour, and they began to shout for him. As the sun sank into the horizon, Nai Khanom Dtom stood alone in the arena. Twelve of Burma's finest fighters lay dead in the settling dust of the great stadium. The king had no alternative but to allow the great Thai fighter his freedom. To this day, muay Thai fighters the world over honour this great hero by dedicating one night of fighting each year to him.

Because of muay Thai's fiercely aggressive nature, it took many years for it to develop even a smattering of rules and regulations. Boxers usually fought in bare feet with their hands gloved in coarse hemp rope, to resemble a type of early boxing glove. Quite often the more devious fighter would mix ground glass with a resin and soak the hemp rope in the mixture, letting it dry out overnight. The next day the unsuspecting opponent would be cut to ribbons. There were few techniques that a fighter was not allowed to use. The famous killer elbow technique was employed on numerous occasions and consequently many deaths resulted. The fighters used coconut shells as groin protectors, which were often split due to the ferocity and force of the fighters' powerful kicks.

Without a doubt the Thai fighter's most valuable close-range attack is the sok or elbow strike. It is a very powerful and dangerous technique. It was because of uncontrolled elbow blows to the head, especially the temple, that most of the deaths occurred in the ring. The elbow is the body's natural battering ram and is capable of delivering tremendous force at a particular target. Its pointed striking area adds increased potency to the applied technique.

In 1931 this fighting art became a national sport and rules were introduced, as were stringent safety measures. The so-called 'death strike' of the elbow to the temple was banned, as was the knee strike into the testicles. Prior to this, fighters often suffered from smashed groins.

Muay Thai spread to the West and its popularity increased. This was probably due to the enlivened interest of Western martial artists in contact sports. Today muay Thai is practised all over the world. It is in Holland, Great Britain, France and Germany that most of the western champions are based.

The secret rites

Muay Thai fighters are incredibly superstitious and place an unshakable belief in the use of good luck charms and talismans. These amulets, they believe, will protect them from harm in the ring and also aid them in their victory. Many fighters place a leaf under their tongue before a fight. This practise is quite common and supposed to endow the fighter with a thick skin, thus protecting him from heavy kicks and blows. Another good luck charm is an arm band called a kruang rang, usually a piece of braid or cord. Underneath it is concealed a miniature figure of the Buddha, indicating that he fights with them during the bout. The Thai people are devout Therevada Buddhists and pay all due respect and homage to their lord. They pray for victory before a fight and pray afterwards as well, whether they win or lose.

At one time it was strictly forbidden for women to enter the ring, their presence allegedly bringing bad luck. But due to the tremendous participation of women in the sport in recent years, this chauvinistic attitude has been waived and is now only aimed at females who are not fighters.

Before a fight begins, every boxer performs a ritualistic dance called ram muay. This ritual is accompanied by music consisting of cymbals, drums and jawa flutes. These dances are extremely important and no fighter would even consider beginning a bout without first going through this ritual. Every training camp—and there are about 800 of these in Thailand—has its own dance; therefore when watching a fighter perform his ram muay it is possible to identify his camp. The movements are executed with a slowly gyrating motion. The fighter first salutes the audience and then begins a series of gestures aimed at the opponent. He will (depending upon his camp) hurl an imaginary spear, then assume that the missile has killed the opponent, begin to dig a grave and finally bury his adversary. All of this is supposed to instil fear into the heart of the opponent, while building up the performer's confidence. When the dance is finished, the fighter walks to his respective corner and bows his head before his teacher, who utters a short prayer for victory and then blows three times at the fighter's forehead. This is known as the 'breath of Buddha'.

The bando system of Burma

Thailand's neighbour, Burma, has a martial art called bando, which means 'way of the disciplined'. The art is based upon twelve animals and practitioners usually select attributes of one or more of these animals and then train in that particular system. For example in the cobra style lie all the lightning-like paralysing nerve strikes. The tiger system extols the ferocity and fighting

Below A high roundhouse kick finds its target in this Thai boxing match. In this case, the striking area is the instep.

power of that animal, whereas the boar form is famous for its hard locking techniques and close-in fighting tactics; modern boar practitioners lay claim that they can fight in a telephone box. Bando was first introduced to the West by a Burmese doctor named Maung Gyi in 1959. Although the art is native in origin and is said to date back many hundreds of years, it is only in recent times, since World War II, that it has gained any kind of prominence.

It is a complete martial system which also incorporates weapons with exotic-sounding names. It is perhaps interesting to note that some of the unarmed methods bear similarities to Thai boxing and also to muay Khmer, the boxing style of neighbouring Cambodia. For instance, many of the kicks in bando are delivered with the shin.

The system does have an underlying philosophy which seems to create a balance between practical results and inner qualities of humility. The breathing techniques of bando are very different from those of other martial arts. For instance in karate a strike is delivered with an exhalation of breath. Bando practitioners prefer to exhale the breath gradually during the execution of a technique. This way they feel they can extend a blow for a longer duration, therefore causing the maximum amount of pain which inhibits an opponent's recovery.

In the boar system, practitioners spend long hours perfecting what they term the 'boar gaze'. Students stare at a lighted candle in a darkened room or pick a spot on a wall and gaze at it continually. This kind of training is meant to emphasize the importance of a strong concentration and will. If the eyes wander, then so will the mind, which leads to defeat. In practice the stare unnerves an opponent.

The Malaysian art of bersilat

Bersilat is an ancient Malaysian art of self-defence, dating back to the early part of the fifteenth century. Today this art is generally referred to simply as silat. It consists of many diverse forms which are also widespread throughout Indonesia. The art developed in the agricultural areas, where most of its instructors lived and worked. It was introduced to Malaysia by the legendary hero and acknowledged father of bersilat, Hang Tuah of Malacca. Hang Tuah is said to have gone into the mountains for several years in search of a maha-guru (a grandmaster) to teach him the skills of this once most secret martial art. The knowledge he acquired through his vigorous training taught him how to face an enemy and defeat him.

It was such a secret martial art in the old days, that in many villages the inhabitants could live their whole lives without ever realizing that a guru or master of silat lived and trained among them. Silat, like many of the martial arts, delves deep into the spiritual aspects. Gayong, one of the major styles means 'pure body and soul', which indicates that the practitioners must be physically and mentally clean. Harimau, the other major style means 'tiger'. A basic tenet of the system is that fighters must never over-estimate their own capabilities.

Silat practitioners always stress that the art should not be used for initiating an attack. It is strictly for self-defence and for counter-attacking when one is in danger. A skilful silat fighter can pin-point with deadly accuracy the 12 vital spots or critical nerve centres on the human body. These are known as seni sendi and can be struck to cause severe pain at the slightest touch of an expert's hand. The assailant will experience a tremendous jolt through his body, reacting as though he had just suffered a severe electric shock.

Malaysian silat incorporates many ground techniques and caters for the possibility of a defender being knocked to the floor and having to counter from a supine position. The most effective ground attack is to cripple the attacker's supporting leg by smashing his kneecap or groin. As soon as they feel themselves falling, students learn to lash out with a type of short side kick.

More than 100,000 people have trained in silat in Malaysia over the past 20 years. At one time, due to its religious aspects, only Muslims were allowed to practise the art, but it is now opening up to Europeans.

The uniform that the practitioner wears is a plain black short-sleeved cotton Malay shirt, with half-length black trousers, and a strip of black cloth tied around the student's forehead. As in the Japanese martial arts, a student's progress in silat is denoted by the wearing of a coloured belt (beng-kong). It takes approximately eight years for the student to gain his black belt in the art. The higher echelons of silat believe that the proper standards have to be maintained at all times and every black belt holder is constantly studied and watched for bad behaviour or personality flaws. Should deficiencies arise, he is forbidden to progress further in the advanced techniques.

Above *Part dance, part martial art, two exponents of capoeira display their skills in Salvador, Brazil.*

The capoiera of Brazil

One of the most overlooked martial arts in the world is that of Brazil's capoiera. This art was born out of slavery, in personal defence of cruelty and persecution. Capoiera was invented by the blacks to fight the vicious slave owners and had its most terrifying results in the slave uprisings. For centuries the blacks kept their art alive under a sworn oath of secrecy. The authorities refused to recognize that such an art ever existed, because if they did, it would attest to the ability of blacks to fight back, thus causing further unrest and insurrection.

Many of the movements are highly acrobatic in application. Some of the foot striking techniques are delivered as the fighter performs a cartwheel on his hands. It is believed that the origins of the art lie in certain African folk dances and that the choreography was altered and adapted to suit the purposes of self-defence. It was through these dances that the slaves managed to hide the lethal aspects of this martial art from the landowners.

In 1965 the Brazilian government recognized capoiera as a native art form and consequently accepted it as a sport, albeit somewhat reluctantly. One of the greatest teachers of capoiera was Master Bimba, who, aided by an anthropologist named Benjamin Muniz, pieced together the various movements of the capoiera dance-cum-martial art and formulated it into a type of long kata to aid students in their instruction. For many reasons the government kept a close watch on its modern development because official thinking always identified the art with rebellion and with the anti-social elements of Brazilian society. Capoiera had been outlawed for over 200 years and its re-introduction in modern times as part of the native cultural heritage was met with fierce opposition.

In capoiera the emphasis is on muscular strength combined with joint flexibility and rapid movement. Making use of very fast body reaction the capoiera fighter can deliver a blow with his feet that could smash a man's internal organs. In a fraction of a second he flips his body over, in a type of handstand, and delivers with tremendous force and accuracy a double-foot blow to the aggressor's body that could well nigh cut him in two. Without a doubt a capoiera man's feet are his deadliest weapons. He trains to kick as most martial artists train to punch. It has been said of capoiera, that it is one of the dirtiest formalized fighting styles known.

Over the last two centuries capoiera has become widespread throughout South America. In the late 1970s it was taken to the USA by a student of the great Master Bimba, Bira Almeida.

As with most martial arts, legends abound. Stories circulate of how in the old days capoiera fighters used to tape knives and razors to their bare feet before entering a fight. In Rio de Janeiro police tried to arrest a capoiera man who had become drunk. Apparently this master of the art despatched nearly two dozen of them before he was finally subdued by force of the gun. On another occasion a 72 year-old capoiera master was accosted in the street by a gang of sailors. Eye witness accounts state that they had barely knocked him to the ground when the old man suddenly sprang into action. His feet scythed into the attackers, cutting them down like ninepins. When the police arrived, the old man had disappeared, leaving in his wake twelve sailors in desperate need of hospitalization.

Capoiera is not a complicated martial art. It has little more than 72 defined separate movements. Many of its techniques have colourful titles such as 'tail of the dragon fish', 'daddy's scissors' and 'banana plant'. Just like martial arts the world over, capoiera had one prime function: it was invented to kill.

The Filipino art of kali

The Philippines are a collection of islands in the South China Sea. For hundreds of years these islands had experienced foreign invasion, from the Moors to the Americans. The native islanders absorbed many martial techniques and incorporated them into their own ancient indigenous art of kali. The name kali comes from the native word kalis, meaning blade or knife. The Muslim Filipinos, known as the Moros, were experts in this specialized martial art. Kali is both an armed and unarmed martial system and, strangely, a beginner learns to use the weapons first and the unarmed self-defence last. One weapon is a native knife known as a bolo, which is very similar to a machete. The Moro warrior fought with a bolo in one hand and a dagger in the other.

Kali has many variations and one of them has been eagerly adopted by western martial artists. This is the art of escrima, which is fought utilizing two hardwood sticks or rattan canes. Escrima is also known by its Spanish term *arnis de mano* meaning 'harness of the hand'. One of the first Europeans to experience the wrath of the kali fighters was Ferdinand Magellan, the great explorer, who in 1521 invaded the island of Cebu, 700 miles (112 km) south of Manila in the Philippines. The Moro tribesmen under the leadership of Lapu Lapu defeated the Spanish landing party, who were armed with swords and guns, with their double hardwood sticks using the art of escrima. This resulted in the death of Magellan.

As invader after invader attempted to subjugate the Filipinos, the fierce Moro tribesmen studied these foreign fighting methods and included them into their own art of kali. There are many styles of Filipino stick fighting because each of the islands developed their own particular methods. The one common denominator is that all these arts are based upon a pattern of angles, regardless of the weapon or style. All the footwork in escrima works along the lines of a triangle, so that an escrimador (one who trains in escrima) can never be trapped or cornered.

During the 300 years of Spanish colonization, the art went underground and was practised in secret, as the Spanish, like the Japanese on Okinawa, had banned all weapons and practice of the martial arts. The Filipinos disguised their art in a dance form that was a particular favourite of the Spanish occupation forces. This dance form was none other than arnis de mano. Throughout the centuries that Spaniards stayed in the Philippines, they were constantly harassed by the guerrilla tactics of the Moro tribesmen.

Spanish rule in the Philippines was followed by American domination of the islands in the early part of this century. The American marines, armed with superior firepower provided by modern technology, found great difficulty in overcoming the Moros. While the rest of the Philippines laid down their arms, the Moros refused to succumb. The US general in charge of the occupying army was General 'Black Jack' Pershing. The losses he suffered from troops having their throats cut were so great that he issued a special leather neck covering to help reduce the casualties among his men. This is why the US marine corps are known as 'leathernecks'. The US campaign against the island natives proved to be quite a struggle. An air of religious fervour was adopted by the Muslim warriors as the Roman Catholic Church on the islands grew in strength. As though in a trance Moro warriors would walk into US occupied towns and armed with either twin sticks or double blades, cut

KALI

I Armed with similar weapons, the attacker (on the right) hits out at his opponent with his stick. It is blocked and then countered by the defender, who makes a cut to the hand with his knife. This technique is known as an inside sweep.

down everyone in their path. One story relates that an American marine corps captain stood in front of a crazed Moro and pumped a full magazine of .38 calibre bullets into him. The Moro took the lot, then decapitated the soldier before dying himself. This incident prompted the US army to issue troops with the .45 calibre pistol, a gun that had much more stopping power. It is something of a mystery whether the Moros were ever beaten. Pershing managed to stop the raids, but the Moro people today still retain their fierce independence and Muslim religion.

With the advent of World War II and the Japanese invasion of the Philippines, many natives rushed to enlist in the US forces, but the Filipino enlistees were not familiar with modern armaments and had great difficulty in conforming to army regulation unarmed combat. After much haggling between the Filipino leaders and the army chiefs, they were allowed to demonstrate their own indigenous arts of kali and escrima. Part of the demonstration involved disarming a dozen or so of the marines' top combat instructors, which they did with great ease. As a result the Filipinos were issued with bolos (knives) to wage a particularly vicious guerrilla warfare campaign against the Japanese.

After the war many Filipinos settled in southern California rather than return home. It was here that escrima, as we know it today, came to the fore.

The Filipino martial art of kali and its offshoot, escrima or arnis, are always presented as stick or blade arts. But kali is very much a complete martial art. Nothing need be added to improve its combat

2 The defender snakes his arm over the attacker's stick.

3 Twisting under and up, he is half way to trapping the attacker's weapon.

4 But the attacker thrusts his dagger at the defender, who quickly snakes his hand around the attacker's other arm, the one holding the dagger.

5
He now locks both the stick and dagger of the attacker, so that he is effectively trapped.

6
Finally the defender places his own dagger at the throat of his would-be assailant, to bring about a submission.

the long and short stick. They figured that if a student became really adept at long and short sticks, to the extent that he could use the sticks at long range, intermediate range and close range, he could also use the dagger together with one of those sticks at the three ranges. The student can then learn to lock, throw, strangle, choke or ground fight with the long and short sticks against someone else with the same weapons. At the same time he will have mastered the single stick because the principles are the same as the double. Additionally, he will understand the principles of the double daggers. If he understands two daggers then he understands one dagger. If he understands one dagger then he understands the empty hands.

Masters or gurus of the art advance the theory that a person cannot enter a fight with pre-set ideas of how they are going to respond with attack and defence. The action is always very fast and the combat ranges are altering all the time, so the kali fighter has to know how to adapt to every situation. He has to be able to flow from one technique into another and become effective at a range that has not been chosen for him. To do this it is not necessary to understand thousands of techniques or several different styles, but simply to understand the principles of motion. Not being bound by one particular method of combat allows the kali fighter to interpret the action as he sees fit. It is perhaps the adaptability of kali that has endeared it to the modern martial artist. This fighting system was born out of the need of the Filipino people to adapt to each new culture that invaded them time and time again, in order to survive. So techniques and training methods were constantly being changed. Kali, as a workable martial art and self-defence system, has survived for hundreds of years because of the fact that it is totally 100 per cent effective.

Russian sambo wrestling

Russian sambo wrestling has developed from many sources. The most distinct contribution has come from the country's central Asian provinces, where sport wrestling has been very popular for hundreds of years. It is believed that the wrestling methods found in central Oriental Russia were culled from the influence of Chinese ch'in-na many centuries previously. Ch'in-na is the art of seizing an opponent by his limbs and throwing him to the ground. It used to be known as a bone-twisting,

effectiveness and nothing can be taken away. Once understood and mastered, the theory prepares the student to meet all possible situations spontaneously.

Kali differs from most other martial arts in that it prefers the student to adapt the system to suit himself, rather than the student having to suit the system. Instructors liken kali to a circle, and a beginner can enter into the art at any point within that circle. If, for instance, a person who is not very strong wants to learn this martial art, he can come in through a training called hubud lubud; this is a sensitivity exercise similar to Wing Chun's chi sau. After learning this he can then go on to study any other area of the martial art from within the kali circle.

Traditionally the old masters taught kali in twelve categories, usually beginning with

Above *These Russian sambo players are clearly enjoying the contest between two of their colleagues. A popular sport in the Soviet Union, it is still little known in the rest of the world.*

sinew-dividing art. In 1936 a prominent Russian wrestler named Anatoly Harlampief decided to do research into many of his country's folk wrestling methods and combine them into a system not seen anywhere else in the world. The result of his endeavours was sambo.

When demonstrations given by sambo men were witnessed, Japan's judo fraternity claimed that Harlampief had merely copied about 75 per cent of judo's techniques and incorporated them into a few indigenous Russian methods that he happened to know. But in 1938 the Soviet Union's national sports committee officially accepted sambo wrestling as an authentic martial art and part of the Russian national heritage and as such they designated it as a bona fide sport.

Although Russian sambo appears to consist of an assorted collection of wrestling methods, it has proved its worth on countless occasions on the mat. Sambo is a combination of two main styles that can be found in the Caucasus and central Asia. One of these specializes in throwing techniques from a standing position, and the other in ground techniques using locks and holds. The word sambo is a Russian acronym from 'self-defence without arms'. It has about 60 basic techniques.

In sambo the wrestler can grip the belt of an opponent, but this is not permitted in judo. Another favourite hold is the back of the jacket and belt. The usual objects of attack are the ankle, knee, wrist and elbow. Pressure holds are applied to intensify pain and force the opponent to submit, which he

does by shouting 'yetsugi'. In competition, there must always be a winner; there are no such things as draws or going into extra time. If both competitors have gained equal points at the end of a bout, then the match is judged by which fighter was the most aggressive.

It is perhaps interesting to note that there are over a quarter of a million active practitioners of sambo in Russia, compared with less than 100,000 judoka.

Kalaripayit—the art of India

Kalaripayit is a martial art practised in both the north and south of India and its name means 'battlefield training'. The art is split into two distinct styles which have gone their separate ways. In the south, kalaripayit's stamping ground is in Kerala province and is mainly practised by the Tamils, while in the northern part of India this fighting art adopts a much harder training regimen. Its adepts are the decendants of the Nayers, who were a great and ferocious warrior caste. The participants train in a practice area called a kalari.

The northern system, which has incredibly high kicking techniques and foot-sweeping manoeuvres, is deeply rooted in religious beliefs. Most masters of the art perform a double function, acting as both a martial arts instructor and the local doctor. The medicine they practise is the traditional Indian ayurvedic system. This involves deep massage of a patient's body, along with the use of herbs and drugs to facilitate recovery. Found in the training regimen of the northern system, are deep-breathing exercises based upon the country's yoga systems. The uniform that practitioners wear is a type of loin-cloth 40 feet (12m) in length. It is donned by the students wrapping one end around a palm tree and winding themselves into it from the other end. Its practical purposes is to act like a truss, protecting the groin and pelvic bone.

The art identifies itself with Kali, the goddess of war, and also the legendary founder of the cult of Thugee, which was an anti-British organization bent upon ridding India of the English. In the latter part of the nineteenth century Thugee gangs, many of whom were kalaripayit disciples, sneaked into the English barracks and homes to strangle their victims silently with a silken scarf which had an Indian rupee encased within its folds. The coin pressed violently against the larynx and choked the unsuspecting victim to death. The English

Right Leaps and flying foot attacks are part of the repertoire of the kalaripayit practitioner.

word 'thug' is derived from this gruesome Indian cult.

Both the northern and southern styles have four main branches attached to the art. These are unarmed training, selambam training (stick fighting), weapon arts and lastly a secret art that only the most advanced students were allowed to learn, called marma-adi. This final part of the training involves attacking the vital points of the body, and resuscitation methods. Because of the tremendous suppleness of

the kalaripayit practitioners, they can execute blocks and attacks from a position almost like sitting. Low postures are performed for ducking under attacks or avoiding strikes. From a crouching position the practitioner can leap several feet in the air twisting his kicks and strikes outwards, thus catching an opponent unawares and battering his body with an onslaught of foot attacks. The fighter can land in a crouch or even a complete leg splits; his legs can then sweep outwards taking his attacker off balance and on to the floor.

Some of the techniques are quite unique to kalaripayit. A great variety of strange and lethal-looking weapons are trained with after the students have mastered the basic techniques. One particular weapon of war is the urumi, a type of coiled spring sword that has four very thin steel bands acting as blades, each of which is double-sided and razor sharp. It is used in a whip-like fashion and upon contact with the bare flesh of the human body can completely strip it of skin in seconds.

Kalaripayit is mostly a village art and is not seen in the industrial areas of India. Its origins are vague, but interestingly many of the postures can be found in the Indian classical dance and the basic fighting position is often seen portrayed in statues of the Indian God Krishna which were carved nearly 4,000 years ago. Today more than one million Indians still train in the indigenous martial art of their homeland.

La savate—the kicking art of France

La savate is a French martial art chiefly concerned with fighting with the feet. The hand movements, apart from the open palms slapping the opponent across the face, hardly exist. There is no guard formed with both fists, as in western and Thai boxing. Unlike Brazilian capoiera, where acrobatics are implemented to effect delivery of attack, savate uses multiple kicks that are applied so incredibly fast, the opponent hardly notices the first two or three actually going in. These kicks are executed from an upright position.

La savate is distinctly different from *la boxe française*, which is the traditional form of French boxing. It is thought that the latter developed from savate in 1830. La savate was a vicious type of fighting used primarily by ruffians and the French footpads (muggers). One of the greatest teachers of the art was a Parisian named Michel Pisseux. The system concentrates on using low kicks to adversary's shins, groin and knees. The few high kicks involved in savate are all targeted upon the head, attacking the eyes, nose and upper lip. An expert in the art can deliver a series of kicks in excess of 30 miles (48km) per hour. All the kicks are applied with clinical precision. The feet move so fast, that even if a technique were to miss its target, another one would follow in just as quickly, giving the opponent very little time to retaliate. The savate man does not rely upon power in technique, because of the sensitive target areas.

It is something of a mystery as to how la savate began in the western city of Paris, as the art bears all the hallmarks of an Oriental origin. It is known that Napoleon, while in exile on Elba, had sent a fact-finding mission to Asia to investigate, among other things, how the native Okinawans had fought so successfully against their Japanese invaders with just their bare hands. Other schools of thought harbour the theory that sailors brought rudiments of Chinese martial arts systems back home with them after their long journies to the Far East. These methods were taken up by ruffians and criminals and used accordingly. Ironically, it is largely due to these low-life developments that la boxe française now exists, although the style includes elements of English boxing with the French foot fighting. La savate is the only martial art with Asian origins that developed in Europe before the advent of judo, nearly 100 years later. To-day, la savate and la boxe française are enjoying a revival in Paris, with schools in Britain and America.

The modern eclectic systems of martial arts

In the early part of this century the Japanese martial arts began to emerge on a world-wide scale, with much interest being shown by western societies in these empty-handed systems of fighting and unarmed combat. For nearly three-quarters of a century the eastern masters dominated these martial arts, but western advances in sports coaching and scientific research into training methods, including psychology, have brought the western martial artist very much to the fore. The old traditional way of training have been re-examined by the logical western mind, to enquire whether, perhaps, through a certain amount of borrowing from several sources the perfect

Right *Because the target has moved, this left jab fails to connect, but it is immediately converted into a powerful forearm and elbow strike to the side of the head. Just one of the techniques being used today in the modern eclectic systems of martial arts.*

Above *Mugendo is an eclectic martial art taken from karate and western boxing. Seen here is an example of the left hook to the jaw.*

martial arts system could be found. The 1980s have seen a considerable amount of this kind of amalgamation.

Such systems are termed 'eclectic' and in effect are a mixture of many different methods of fighting. Martial arts instructors, themselves having been well grounded in Oriental methods, have combined western boxing with taekwon-do kicking power, or the throws of jiu-jitsu with the fluidity of kung fu and renamed their efforts with, ironically enough, an Eastern-sounding title. Whether this is a good thing, only time will tell. But picking the best parts and techniques from other disciplines and then renaming them under a new system almost certainly leaves behind the original intentions. As we have seen throughout this book, each of the martial arts has an underlying philosophy running through it. This was to be the code for behaviour and, very often, a complete way of life. Eclectic

martial arts systems seem to be devoid of any such philosophical principles. They appear to be orientated towards the street, where it is a case of the trained fighter versus the mugger, in an all-out, life or death struggle for survival. The traditional martial arts held in one hand a complete fighting system and in the other hand a school of philosophical thought. The two were meant to run side by side, each complementing the other.

Wars are no longer fought at an individual level; more often than not the enemy dies without ever seeing the man who killed him. Gone are the days when two samurai met face to face upon the battlefield to fight for honour and justice, or warriors armed with spear and sword battled it out steel against steel, when the victor was the man with the highest amount of skill and courage. Modern warfare does not allow sportsmanlike conduct or individualism on the battlefield. The glory of death means very little to the modern soldier.

In ancient China the kung fu master could easily beat multiple armed assailants, by using his bare-handed skills. Two thousand years on the modern martial arts master, faced with a similar situation, would come up against modern technology—the firearm. No martial arts system exists that can successfully stop or block a bullet. So then, bearing all this in mind, why does anyone actually learn a martial art? The answer to that is the same as it was 2,000 years ago: to breed a better person, a person who can develop a deeper understanding of the self and of his or her environment, and who can seek what is good in others rather than be perpetually in direct contention. Through the training and philosophies offered by the martial arts that person can build up a greater confidence. This confidence spills over into daily life and he or she is more able to cope with life's day-to-day problems. The trained, physically fit martial artist reacts to adverse situations in a different manner from the average person in the street. The training prepares all students spiritually, emotionally, mentally and psychologically for life's little pitfalls and how best to overcome them.

The martial arts are not just composed of fighting techniques; they represent a whole way of life, an on-going process of individual development, that has not changed in over 2,000 years. The words of an old Chinese proverb put it succinctly: 'Give me a fish and I am fed for a day; teach me to fish and I am fed for a lifetime.'

GLOSSARY

Acupuncture Chinese system of healing using needles at key points of the body.

Age-uke Rising block (karate).

Atemi Japanese for the vital points of the body, which when attacked can cause pain, injury or even death.

Black belt The level of proficiency in martial arts at which a student may graduate to instructor.

Bokken or **bokuto** A wooden sword used for training in Japanese martial arts.

Buddhism Asian religion founded by the Indian philosopher Gautama, 5th c. BC.

Bushi Japanese warrior who followed the code of bushido, stressing honour, loyalty, duty and obedience.

Cat stance Used in kung fu and karate, the weight is placed on the back leg.

Centreline The imaginary line of Wing Chun kung fu which runs down the centre of the body, the focus of attack and defence.

Ch'an Chinese for Zen, or meditation.

Chi Internal force or energy which is harnessed in particular by practitioners of tai chi chuan and hsing-i.

Chi sao The exercising of Wing Chun kung fu to develop sensitivity in the arms.

Chudan The chest area of Japanese martial arts.

Dan Japanese for degree, denoting rank of black belt.

Dim mak Death touch, or strike to a vital point causing delayed injury or death.

Dit da jow Chinese herbal ointment used to prevent bruising during training.

Do Japanese for path or way, also used as a suffix, eg kendo.

Dobok Korean for practice suit.

Do jang Korean for training hall.

Dojo Japanese for training hall.

Dohyo The mound on which sumo matches are played.

Empi Japanese for elbow.

Escrima Spanish for 'skirmish'. Filipino system employing sticks, swords and daggers.

Five Ancestors Survivors of the sacking of the Shaolin temple, credited with founding the Triad societies.

Five Animals Movements of the crane, dragon, leopard, tiger and snake incorporated into the Shaolin fighting systems.

Form see Kata.

Gedan-barai Downward block (karate).

Gi Training uniform for Japanese martial arts. In Korean it means spirit.

Gup In taekwon-do one of the ten grades below black belt.

Gyaku-zuki Reverse punch (karate).

Gyoji Sumo referee.

Haito Ridge-hand (karate).

Hakama Long divided skirt used in some Japanese martial arts, notably aikido and kendo.

Hara-kiri Japanese ritual suicide by disembowelment, the ultimate act of atonement whereby a samurai could regain his lost honour.

Heian The name given to the five basic karate katas.

Horse stance Strong basic stance of both Chinese and Japanese styles.

Iga Remote region of medieval Japan where the ninja lived and trained.

I Ching Ancient Chinese book of divination, whose philosophical principles form the basis of tai chi, pa-kua and hsing-i.

Ippon Used in Japanese contests to denote a full point.

Jodan The face area of Japanese martial arts.

Judoka One who practises judo.

Jutsu or **jitsu** Japanese for skill or art, also used as a suffix, eg kenjutsu.

Karate-ka One who practises karate.

Kata A pattern or form of moves in which the Japanese martial artist fights imaginary opponents.

Katana A Japanese sword.

Keage Snap kick (karate).

Kekomi Thrust kick (karate).

Ki Japanese for chi (q. v.), internal energy vital to the practice of aikido and hapkido.

Kiai Powerful shout of Japanese martial arts which can stun an opponent or give extra impetus to a technique.

Kiba-dachi The straddle-leg or horse-riding stance of karate.

Kihon Basic training techniques of Japanese martial arts.

Kobudo Ancient Japanese warrior ways.

Kote Kendo gauntlet.

Kumite Japanese for sparring.

Kup so Vital spot in taekwon-do.

Kizami-zuki Jab (karate).

Kokutsu-dachi Back stance (karate).

Kwoon Chinese for training hall.

Kyu Japanese for any grade below shodan (1st degree black belt).

Martial arts The arts of war, from Mars, the Roman god of war.

Ma-ai Correct distancing when faced with an opponent.

Mae-geri Karate front kick.

Makiwara Punching board.

Men Kendo helmet.

Mawashi-geri Roundhouse kick.

Mook joong Wooden dummy used for conditioning in many hard kung fu styles.

Newaza Grappling techniques.

Nukite Karate spear hand.

Oi-zuki Karate lunge punch.

Oos Form of greeting used in the dojo (q. v.).

Pattern see Kata.

Randori Free sparring of judo.

Ronin A samurai without a master.

Ryu Japanese for school or style.

Samurai 'One who serves'—the knightly warrior of feudal Japan.

Sanchin-dachi Hour-glass stance.

Sensei Japanese for master.

Shiatsu Japanese finger pressure therapy.

Shinai Bamboo sword made of four strips bound together. Replaces the live blade in kendo.

Shinto Japanese animalistic religion, also based on ancestor worship. It means 'way of the gods'.

Shuto Knife hand in karate.

Sifu A kung fu master.

Sil Lum Cantonese for the Shaolin temple.

Soto-uke Outside block with the wrist (karate).

Sweep A foot technique to unbalance the opponent.

Sumotori Sumo wrestlers.

Tachiwaza Throwing techniques.

Tachiai The first moment of contact in a sumo match.

Tanden Japanese for navel, thought to be the source of power.

Taoism 'The right way'—Chinese religious doctrine attributed to Lao-Tse, c. 500 BC.

Tare Apron, part of kendo armour, to protect the vital points below the waist.

Te Okinawan for hand, as in karate (empty hand).

Tenugui Headband used in kendo to absorb perspiration.

Tul A pattern in taekwon-do.

Uchi-uke Inside block of karate.

Ude-uke Forearm block (karate).

Uraken Japanese for back fist.

White belt This denotes beginner in several Japanese systems.

Waza-ari A half point (in Japanese competition).

Yang In Chinese cosmology, the active male principle of the universe, intertwined with yin (q. v.).

Yame Finish—generally denoting the end of a kata.

Yin The passive female principle of Chinese cosmology, intertwined with yang (q. v.).

Yoko-geri Karate side kick.

Yokozuna Rank of grand champion in sumo wrestling.

Yoi Ready position in Japanese martial arts.

Zanshin A state of calm alertness cultivated in Japanese martial arts.

Zen Religious philosophy that claims one can reach satori (enlightenment) through meditation.

Zenkutsu-dachi Forward stance of karate.

INDEX

ACKNOWLEDGMENTS

The author would like to thank the following people for their invaluable assistance: Terry O'Neill of *Fighting Arts* magazine, also Mr David Moore and Maureen Rochford.

Marshall Cavendish are very grateful to the following individuals and organizations for providing expert advice and giving so generously of their time towards the compilation of this book: The British Kendo Association, ℅ The Martial Arts Commission, Broadway House, 15–16 Deptford Broadway, London SE8 4PA; The International Taekwon-do

Federation, ITF Centre, a-1070 Vienna, Stollgasse 8/2, Austria (tel. 222–963035) and All Europe Taekwon-do Federation, 36 Woodberry Avenue, North Harrow, Middlesex HA2 6AX (tel. 01-863 0664); The British Shorinji Kempo Federation, 72 Anson Road, London N7 0AA (tel. 01-607 5931); also to Paul Yip who demonstrated the kung fu techniques for photography, and to Alan Wallace and Jon Pitts, instructors at The Central Karate Club, The Place, 17 Dukes Road, London WC1 (tel. 01-585 2368), who

demonstrated the moves for the Shotokan karate picture sequences.

PICTURE CREDITS
Special photography on behalf of Marshall Cavendish by Roy Victor: 8, 14, 28, 30, 31, 32BL & BR, 33–35, 42, 48, 49, 50TL & TR, 51, 52, 61–66 & 67B. Other acknowledgments are as follows: Anglo-Chinese Educational Institute 44; Mary Evans Picture Library 12; David Finch 93–96, 99; Werner Forman Archive 81, 104; Mark Foxwell 73–77; Norma Harvey 5, 16, 25, 39, 43, 46, 53–58, 60,

68, 69, 78, 85, 86, 90, 91, 122, 124; International Taekwon-do Federation: 114–121; Japan Information Centre 72, 82; Kobal Collection 36–38; Eileen Langsley 97; Peter Lewis 10, 15, 23, 24, 26–27, 32T, 40, 41, 50B, 67T, 79BL, 83, 84, 89, 92, 102, 105–113, 126–128, 131–133, 135–137; Tony Morrison 130; Newnes Group Picture Library (National Palace Museum, Taipei, Taiwan); Novosti Press Agency 134; Victoria & Albert Museum (Michael Holford) 70–71, 100; Wellcome Institute Library, London 13B.